The Triangle

of the Uncaused Cause

Thomas J. Pojeta

Hoot Books Publishing
851 French Moore Blvd.
Suite 136 Box 14
Abingdon, VA 24210

DEDICATION

For the women who helped make me the man I am:
My mother, Rose, who guided me through difficult times;
Zeets, who taught me how to hug and
that it's okay to cry;
Tina, who will always be her Daddy's little girl;
and
Cindy, the second love of my life,
whose encouragement made this book a reality.

Table of Contents

PROLOGUE - SUNRISE

It's dark, quiet, not a hint of movement. I'm on the back porch swing having my first cup of coffee of the day. Every morning I wake up before sunrise and plug in the percolator that Cindy prepared the night before. I pour the steaming brew and add a generous portion of vanilla flavored creamer. Weather permitting, I take that scrumptious coffee— my liquid life— to the back porch swing to slowly wake up and come alive. This is my special time, my precious luxury, to just sit, think, and pray. I start my morning prayers and allow my mind to wander wherever it wishes.

It's very dark and day has not yet broken, but there is illumination from two dusk-to-dawn blue lights, one on each corner of the porch. In the distance, there is a row of blue solar lights on either side of the boat dock that resemble an approach to a landing strip. I chose blue for two reasons: first to repel insects, but also because it's my favorite color. Except for the occasional squeak of the swing, it is very quiet as I gently sway back and forth.

I am retired; there's no urgency in my morning routine of sitting, thinking, swinging, and praying. Day is beginning to break over the tree-covered mountains and there is just enough light to outline the shoreline of the lake below. Across the lake on the far shore are the tree covered mountains of the serene Cherokee National Forest. As it gets lighter the rays of the sun begin to reflect gorgeous color off the wispy clouds. The sun is still concealed behind the horizon. The silence is broken by the birds waking up to greet the day. Two of them have just arrived at the bird feeder filled with a generous mixture of assorted seeds that hangs from the top of the porch on a pivotal arm.

The tempo and volume of chirping intensifies as more and more birds gather. A hummingbird approaches the ruby red nectar filled feeder hanging next to the bird feeder. The eastern sky is resplendent and brighter each moment and its magnificent beauty is reflected off the glass-like surface of the lake.

My wife Cindy, our dog Petey, and our cat Baby Martin come out to join me. I excitedly point out the color of the sky only to be teased that I can't even see how vibrant and incredible the colors are. Cindy reminds me of how much beauty I miss due to my color-weakness, or as she refers to it, color-blindness. Cindy goes into the house and retrieves my color blind glasses and hands them to me saying, "Try these." I put them over my bifocals and look at the sky and am amazed. I ask Cindy to try them and she does but they have no effect on her. The glasses were designed to enhance color perception of the red-green spectrum. I can't explain how they work; however, I am sure the information is available. I am content to enjoy the technology. I am awed by the vast amount of knowledge that exists and the infinite amount of knowledge that is yet to be identified.

Down on the lake, an armada of Canadian geese swim by in search of their morning meeting and feeding location. They are a boisterous flock honking some goose prayer.

We are on the South Houston Lake in Abingdon, Virginia. Soon Cindy and I will make our plan of the day, but for the moment, we simply enjoy the splendor that only God could have made.

Sunrise

1940-1950

A YOUNG BOY

CHAPTER 1
A BABY BOY NAMED TOM

My life began on a rare day in 1940. The next time Holy Thursday will fall on March 21st is 2391. My parents, Jerry and Rose Pojeta, welcomed their first-born: a baby boy weighing 9 pounds.

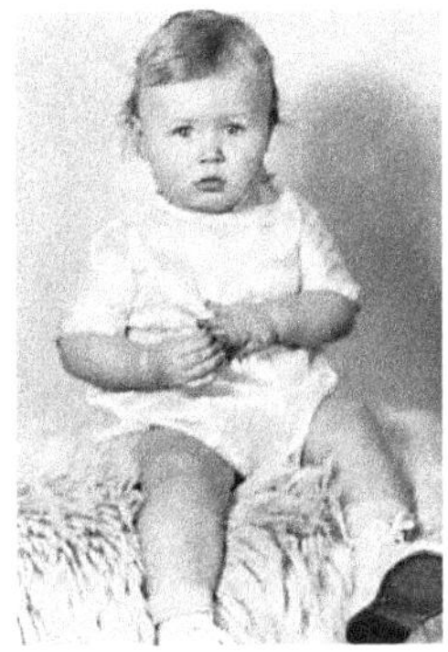

Tom at 6 months old

I assume those first few years of life were simple and rather mundane. However, when I was three years old, I was sitting in a neighbor's doghouse with their collie by my side looking out into a backyard filled with people. My mother was beckoning me to come out. I refused and stayed with my loyal protector, safe from what I perceived was harm. Years later, I was told how and why I ended up huddled with the dog in his house. It was because I settled my squabble with a playmate by hitting him on the head with a hammer. I fled to the doghouse seeking sanctuary as I did not know the extent of his injuries or the nature of my punishment. Thankfully, he was not seriously hurt.

* * * * * *

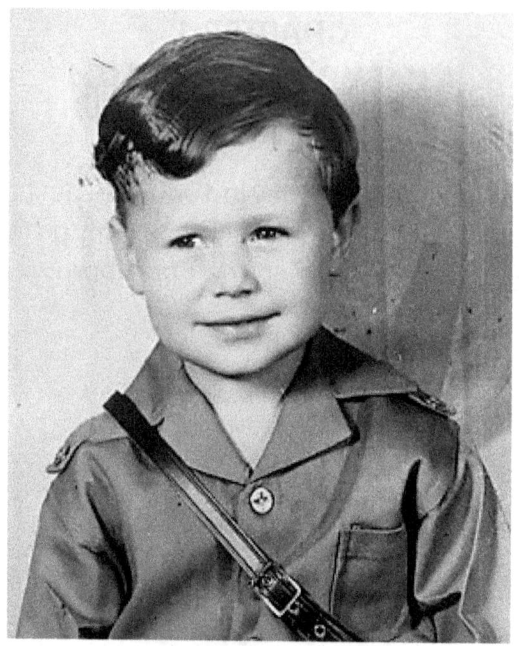

Tom at 3 years old

With the start of WWII there was a demand for highly skilled tool and die makers. My father was successful in convincing a company that he had such skills. This employment exempted him from military service. Unfortunately, his skills did not match his resumé claims. I remember him sharing with my mother his struggles with the mathematical calculations required for the job. My mother assisted the best she could, but ultimately his frustration with the challenges he faced in the workplace caused him to lose the job and strike out on his own. He started a photographic studio although he had no professional experience in photography.

* * * * * *

My family moved several times. We rented houses and at times lived with both sets of grandparents. My paternal grandparents, Frank and Rose Pojeta, lived far away on a farm in Wisconsin. I was at least four years old before I met them. My maternal grandparents, Albert and Mary Bartik, lived nearby, and we would visit them often. One of the best things about their house was the well-stocked refrigerator that always seemed to contain tiny cups of Jello and pudding. I liked the red Jello best. However, nothing could compare to grandma's magic pies, especially apple. It wasn't only that they were delicious, but that she shared the experience of baking them with my siblings and me. I loved to watch her routine from beginning to end. She would remove a big blob of dough from the refrigerator, sprinkle flour on the cutting board and roll the dough flat. Next would come the sweet fruity filling. While she put the top crust on, I had the honor of licking the bowls and spoons clean. The wonderful smell filled the house, and it seemed forever for the pies to cook and even longer for them to cool. It was always worth the wait. No one, including my mother, could ever duplicate the recipe. I can hardly remember a visit to her house that did not include a piece of pie. To this day the aroma of baking pies brings my grandma to mind.

* * * * * * *

When I was six years old, my parents purchased their first house and the photography business seemed successful. I went to the studio with my father to help him clean. The one interesting memory I have of the photography studio is when my father was hired to photograph the cast of the WLS National Barn Dance. He took me along and I got to meet famous performers including Rex Allen, Gene Autry, and Minnie Pearl. Soon I started the first grade at the local Catholic school, Saint Mary of Lasalle. I enjoyed everything about school and my classmates. I was chosen to partake in a pageant honoring the 25th anniversary of our parish priest's ordination. We lived close by the school and when the weather was fair I walked home by myself.

* * * * * * *

Across the street from the school lived two little black dogs in the corner house's backyard. I took great delight running a stick along the fence and teasing them. One day the dogs found a hole in the fence and when I approached to do my mischief, they came out of the yard and chased me. I ran back in the direction of the school with the dogs nipping at my heels. I tried to scale the four-foot-high makeshift cinderblock incinerator for safety. However, as I was climbing, one of the dogs sunk his teeth into my tender little buttocks and hung in midair until he was tired and then they retreated. I lowered myself to the ground and started for home by a different route. I explained to my mom what had happened, and she got the neighbor to drive us to the local clinic for treatment. The clinic called the police and a report was filed. The dogs were quarantined in their house in case I developed rabies, and I received a topical treatment that hurt worse than the bite. I certainly learned my lesson, and from that point on I never taunted the dogs again.

* * * * * * *

As a six-year-old, my life was wonderful. I was living the good life. I played Kick-the-Can in the alley with my neighborhood buddies and went Trick-or-Treating on Halloween. I enjoyed the companionship of our family dog, a black cocker spaniel named Kelly. My sister, who was one year younger than me, was also my faithful playmate. I called her Dodo because I couldn't pronounce her real name, Dorothy. That nickname endured while we were toddlers, but eventually my mom encouraged me to call her Dorothy. I had no idea my life was about to dramatically change.

* * * * * * *

My father was always leaving a job and going to a new occupation. But the one thing he was obsessed with was the idea of returning to a farm. My mother hated the idea and attempted to dissuade him. Whenever he got word of a piece of land up for sale in Illinois, Indiana, Wisconsin, or Michigan he was off and running to scope it out. I was his faithful traveling companion. I didn't mind; I enjoyed the travel. Finally, when I was seven years old and in the middle of second grade, an 80-acre farm in southwest Michigan came up for sale. By then my fourth sister, Judith (Judy) had been born in February 1947. In March 1947, the seven of us (my parents, my sisters Dorothy, Jeanne, Pat, Judy and I) moved to Cassopolis, Michigan. The farm was purchased with the financial help of my father's parents.

* * * * * * *

After moving to the farm, I was enrolled in the second grade at St. Mary's grade school in Niles, Michigan.

Almost immediately my entire class began preparing began preparing to receive the sacrament of Holy Eucharist. At home my mother read stories to me about the beauty and holiness of receiving the Holy Eucharist. My father announced that on the day of my First Holy Communion I would be excused from doing all my chores. Obviously, this was going to be a very important day in my life. At the time, I didn't fully appreciate what a profound impact it would have on the rest of my life. It was the moment when I was permanently coupled to my Supreme Being. Every time since then when I receive the Holy Eucharist, I am in communion with Jesus.

Tom at his first Holy Communion

CHAPTER 2
THE FARM

All the structures— the house, the barn, the chicken coops, the detached garage, the two-hole outhouse— were dilapidated and on the verge of falling down. The house was a two-story frame building with a basement cellar. The first floor had a kitchen, dining room, living room, my parents' bedroom, and a large, enclosed back porch. My father put a four-foot by eight-foot piece of plywood on top of the dining room table and constructed bench seating on one side for the five oldest children. The table was the hub of our family's activities where we did homework, prepared treats for the holidays, and where visiting friends and relatives played Pinochle.

In the corner of the living room, we always put the Christmas tree between the two windows. That was my favorite time of the year because I was allowed to sleep on the sofa while the tree was up. On the north wall was my mom's desk where she kept the household records and did her correspondence and writing. She had a weekly column in the local paper, *The Cassopolis Vigilant* called the "Daily-Edwardsburg Corner." Despite a house full of children and being unable to drive, she used her imagination and education to write entertaining vignettes. Her annual salary was a box of candy at Christmas time.

The room also contained the vacuum-tube radio which I would tune into my favorite station and listen to *The Lone Ranger*. It wasn't until my senior year of high school that we acquired our first television set. It was a very small black and white model that mostly displayed static and snow. Across from the sofa were two stuffed armchairs with the heat duct between them. My father always sat in the one on the left-hand side. When my sisters were dating, my future brothers-in-law would sit in that chair until they saw my father coming, then they would jump out. In the evenings, my father would sit and read and drink his homemade grape wine. There were many barrels of his hooch in the cellar. Most nights he would stagger to bed. I guess I never wanted to label him an alcoholic, but the term probably applies.

In my parents' room under the window was my mother's treadle sewing machine. She used it to mend our clothes and patch my britches. Next to the sewing machine was an over overstuffed chair that was constantly filled with clean clothes that needed repairs. In the corner of the room was my parents' double bed and a crib that never seemed to be empty because of the frequent arrival of siblings.

The second floor had three large rooms and one small room which was at the top of the stairs above my parents' bedroom. To get to the other rooms, it was necessary to walk through the small one. That was my bedroom. Along one wall was a single bed with a nightstand under the window. On the opposite wall there was a homemade table that served as my homework desk and the surface for all my hobbies including painting, woodcarving, and experiments. The next room had three beds and was the girls' room. The last two rooms were storage/junk rooms that we used as closets.

When we first moved in, there was nothing in the house but lightbulbs hanging from the ceiling and a pitcher hand-pump in the kitchen sink which drew water from a cistern. The heating system consisted of a wood and coal fired furnace that heated the living and dining rooms. All the other rooms on the first floor and the bedrooms on the second floor only received heat that flowed up the stairs and through open doors. My bedroom was very cold in those Michigan winters. When it snowed at night, I would wake up to a fine dusting on my bedside table which was next to the window.

The main water source was a well with an electric pump on the enclosed back porch. The water had to be carried in buckets into the house and to other structures. During our first summer, an unground water line was laid from the pump to the kitchen and the barn. Every Saturday night, water was heated on the wood-burning kitchen stove and poured into a metal washtub for all of us children to take a bath. I remember my sisters calling out for the "first after Tom" position. This was a terrible hardship for my mother who was accustomed to city life with all its modern conveniences. About two years later, part of the back porch was converted to a full bathroom. I remember my father and I hitching the team of horses to a wagon and traveling four miles to the railroad station to pick up the bathtub he purchased from the Sears and Roebuck catalog.

The 80-acre farm was divided into two unequal portions separated by a gravel road. Across the road from the house was a ten-acre pond surrounded by a meadow to pasture the cows. During the summer, we children would splash in the cool water. During the winter, we would don our ice skates and play "Fox and Geese" and other games on the ice. The pond also served to water all the livestock. There was a barn with a silo. It had eight stalls for milking cows and four stalls for the working horses. Above the barn was a huge loft for storing loose hay and straw. While most all the time I spent in the barn was hard work, occasionally the other children and I would play in the hay.

* * * * * * *

My father's first procurement as a farmer was 500 baby chicks. He "modified" part of the chicken house and heated it with an oil burning stove to keep the chicks warm. His next purchases were three milking cows and a team of horses. Soon after, on a Sunday morning, my father and I were in the barn doing the morning chores including feeding and milking the cows when he told me to go back to the house to get another pail. As I left the barn and was walking to the house, I saw huge flames coming out the side of the chicken coop and yelled, "Fire!"

My father jumped up from milking a cow and knocked over the pail of milk. He soon realized there was no way to save the chicken house and the hundreds of chicks. He rushed to the car and drove two miles to another farm to phone the volunteer fire department. They arrived in time to contain the fire and prevent it from spreading to the other buildings. As the firefighters battled the blaze, I asked my father a typical seven-year-old child's question: "Can we save any of the chicks?" He responded, "They're all gone." Those chicks were a city boy's first farm animals, but I still saw them as pets. I had helped feed and water them. I felt affection for them and had just lost them. After the embers cooled, I went inside and saw the little bones everywhere.

After the fire, I would not eat chicken. After I graduated from college, I was invited by a neighbor girl to a church barbecue. While in line for dinner, I saw the pieces of chicken on the grill and felt panic. However, I figured everyone was eating it and it wouldn't kill me. Also, I didn't want to offend anyone or embarrass my date. When the cook asked me what I would like I said, "That piece," and pointed to the smallest one. When I tasted it, it was quite good. To this day I will eat chicken, but it is my least favorite meat. A new chicken house was built that summer and restocked with more chicks, but there was never another oil heater, my father purchased an electric one.

* * * * * * *

The first summer on the farm I learned how to work with a team of horses, Dolly and Babe. I followed behind as they pulled a spike-toothed drag, an implement to level plowed ground before sowing grain. We planted corn, wheat, oats, and rye. We planted these for our own subsistence and as feed for the animals. The wheat and rye were ground into flour to make homemade bread and chicken feed. The corn and oats were primarily to feed the cows and horses. A large portion of what we raised, our family ate. If we didn't raise it, we didn't eat it. The soil was very poor and produced meager crops. It would be many years before the land would be a respectable farm, long after I moved away.

Ironically, the one crop that was most successful was the two acres of Concord grapes. While some of them did end up in my mom's jelly and desserts, most were the basis for my father's abundant wine production. My father thought his ruby red concoction was excellent. I tasted it and did not agree. He bragged about it and insisted every visiting friend and relative sample it. Everyone tried to resist but eventually ended up being gracious guests and accepting a glass. Most often, as soon as my father was not in sight, the wine ended up watering my mother's house plants.

* * * * * *

Shortly after entering third grade, one of our three cows stepped into a gopher hole and broke her hip. I recall my father trying to nurse her and after a few days heard him tell my mother the cow could not be saved. One day while I was at school, my parents butchered her. Every time I went into the barn and saw her empty stall I was sad and missed her. It was difficult to eat her, and it caused me to dislike beef for many years.

* * * * * *

That first winter on the farm, it seemed like the snow started earlier and there was much more of it than in Chicago. One night, after we were all in bed, my father called for me to get up. I went downstairs and there was a strange lady in the dining room. My father told me she was returning home from a Tupperware party, her car slid off the road into a ditch, and we needed to harness the horses and pull her out. He told me to dress and meet him in the barn. While my father went to the barn, the lady started walking back toward her car. My mother bundled me up in lots of layers of clothes, boots, a hat, gloves, and scarf.

The horses were frisky. They had not had any exercise for several weeks. They seemed to delight in trudging down the road through twelve inches of newly fallen snow. My father and I walked behind the horses for about a quarter of a mile to the bend in the road where the car had slid into the ditch. The lady was in the car with the engine running and the lights on. My father attached a logging chain to the car and the horses had no trouble pulling it out. He told the lady to drive back to the house and as she started to drive, she immediately slid back into the ditch. The horses pulled the car out again and my father drove the car towards our house. He told me to take the horses back to the barn.

The two reins were attached together and went under my arms and around my back. All went well at first, but about halfway back, the horses realized the warm barn was not far away and began to gallop. I could not keep up with them, and I could not free myself. My feet gave way and the team dragged me face first through the snow. The snow slammed into my face and under my clothes. My father heard the horses coming and ran out to the road to stop them. He untangled me from the reins and brushed away some snow. He told me to go into the house while he took the horses to the barn. As my mother undressed me, a big pile of snow fell on the floor. She bathed my skin with rubbing alcohol to stimulate my blood flow because she feared I had frostbite. My parents convinced the lady to spend the night rather than risk driving off the road again. My mother gave her bedding and she slept on the couch. The next morning after breakfast when the snowplow had cleared the road, she departed.

CHAPTER 3
TRIXIE AND CHERRY

In December 1948, I got a little brown puppy. Friends of the family who lived nearby had a dog which had a litter, and they were trying to find homes for them. My parents were not enthusiastic about getting a puppy, but after a considerable amount of "Oh! please" and "Can I please have a puppy?" they acquiesced. I named her Trixie after a dog my maternal grandparents once had that I loved. She was a mixed breed and had the markings of a boxer with a terrier face. My mother refused to have animals in the house unless their lives depended on it. I was able to convince her that I would keep Trixie in a box by my bed just for that first winter. Trixie was lonely in that box and in the middle of the night she would whimper. I would reach down and pick her up and put her under the covers with me. After a short while, she didn't wait for me to lift her but jumped up to snuggle. There was no heat in my bedroom, but we kept each other warm. She grew and became my sole and faithful companion when I was working in the fields and doing chores.

We couldn't afford dog food, and I wasn't allowed to feed her "people" food other than scraps and bones, but she was a great hunter. She was a fast runner and a wild rabbit in the open field had no chance of escape. She had a major problem: occasionally she would kill one of our chickens. After the kill, she would take it to her favorite dining area— the front yard. This infuriated my father, and he threatened to shoot Trixie. I devised to plan to save her. I took her into the woods and tied her to a tree on a long rope and gave her food and water. I visited her several times each day. This went on for two days and gave my father time to calm down.

Another farmer suggested the way to stop a dog from killing chickens was to tie the dead chicken around the dog's neck. I did that, but later the same day, she freed the chicken from her neck and was eating it. Whether that remedy was the reason or not, she never killed another chicken after that day. A few years later, I was in the pig sty separating little piglets from the sow to wean them. The piglets were squealing and the mother sow charged at me. Trixie came flying over the top of the fence and sunk her teeth into the sow. That diversion allowed me to escape. Trixie saved my life.

Trixie and I had a strong and loving bond. She was at my side whenever I was outside and seemed to anticipate whatever I was going to do. I have often expressed to my family and friends my belief that Trixie could read my mind. There were several times that I tested that theory. When out of sight of her and with no audible signaling, I would think of a command, such as "Here Trixie" and she would respond. I was convinced that Trixie and I had a special energy connection. However, the connection only worked in one direction—I was the transmitter, she was the receiver. At times I felt Trixie was trying to transmit to me with her eyes, but I was unable to receive.

Whenever Trixie didn't greet me and accompany me on my morning chores, I knew it could only mean one thing: she had a new litter. She always had her puppies in the same location. I would pass by to congratulate her but give her a few days before entering her "maternity ward" under the barn between two floor joists. I would crawl under the barn to bring her a handful of table scraps which she would devour and then I would take inventory of the new arrivals. She usually had four to six pups each time. If anyone other than me tried to get close to the entrance, they were met with her growls. If that did not deter a trespasser, she would give a more menacing growl, bare her teeth, and the hair on her neck would stand up. I was privileged to come as I pleased and pet her babies. She always seemed so proud and wagged her tail as I played with them. She would come with me and watch over them when I took them out to my sisters who were anxiously waiting beside the barn. We never were allowed to keep any of the puppies and my task was to find good homes for all of them.

* * * * * * *

In our front yard, there was a very large Sugar Maple tree. The tree was spectacular, the foliage in the shape of an inverted heart. In the autumn, it was a breathtaking burst of reds and oranges. The diameter of the branches was bigger than my waist. Often people passing would stop their cars to take pictures of this beauty. Once a lady sat alongside the road in front of her easel and painted the tree on canvas. Occasionally, on pleasant Sunday afternoons, I would climb into its lofty branches and play games like pretending I was Robinson Crusoe. My faithful companion Trixie would lie at the base of the tree awaiting my safe descent. Over sixty years after I left the farm for college, my sister Mary and her husband Paul took Cindy and I to see what had become of the farm. It had been sold years before and was now subdivided into over a dozen homes. Everything I had known was gone. It would have been unrecognizable if it hadn't been for the Sugar Maple still standing in all its splendor.

* * * * * *

Life on the farm was very unpleasant. There was almost no time to play. I worked like an adult hired hand and it caused me to struggle with my schoolwork. In the morning, I woke up around 5 am to milk the cows by hand and feed the animals. After I cleaned up and ate breakfast, my father would drive us children to the school. We attended Saint Mary's, a Catholic elementary school, about 15 miles from the farm. After school, my father would pick us up. Once we were home, my mother would give us a snack and I changed back into my work clothes.

Michigan winters were the worst with temperatures below zero and 20-30 mile an hour winds. When I woke up, my bedroom was freezing cold and my windows rattled. I crawled out of bed, grabbed my clothes and shoes, and headed downstairs where it wasn't much warmer. Luckily, down in the basement was a little better. The coal and wood banked in the furnace the night before was merely embers by dawn. It was my responsibility to get the fire started. I loaded the furnace with wood and coal and was grateful for the first smoke and flames. I sat on the bottom step and dressed and waited for the fire to take hold. Outside, it was always still dark and very cold.

The snow blew into deep drifts making it difficult to walk to the barn while carrying a dim lantern and milking bucket. The two 60-watt light bulbs barely lit the barn. Trixie was always happy to see me. She would rise out of her nest in the straw to greet me. First, I fed each cow a portion of silage with ground grain sprinkled on top. Next, I scraped the cow droppings out of the stalls. We usually had eight milking cows, but in winter months many were pregnant and not producing milk. During the rest of the year there was plenty of milk. I used a hand crank machine to separate the cream from the milk. We sold the cream to a dairy and fed the skim milk to the hogs. But in the winter, there was only enough milk for the family's consumption. During the milking, the three barn yard cats would come near waiting for a squirt of warm milk in their faces. After I hung the milk pail on a nail to keep the cats from stealing it, I watered the cows and put out clean straw.

We barely eked out an existence and it became necessary for my father to seek employment off the farm to support us. He worked second shift for the New York Central railroad. If it was not raining before he left for work, he would harness the horses because I was too small and not strong enough to do it myself. I did field work including harvesting corn by hand and tossing it into a wagon pulled by the team of horses until dark. When I put the horses up at night, I was able to unbuckle the harnesses and slide them to the floor where they would lie until my father came home from work and hung them up. However, if it was raining I couldn't work in the field. I liked rain. After I put the horses up, I had to milk the cows, feed the livestock, and clean out the barn. Around eight or nine at night, I would eat dinner, usually alone as my sisters were already in bed. There was almost no time for homework, and if there was, I was too tired to do it.

There were times when we didn't plant a crop in a field, or it had just been harvested. If the field was not fenced, we would use it for the cows to graze. We children would take turns watching the cows to make sure they didn't wander off our property, especially onto the road. I never minded when I got a turn, although it wasn't often as it was a chore that one of my many sisters could perform. I would take a book and Trixie. To pass the time, I would build something out of sticks and rocks and mud, but sometimes, I would read.

Trixie would amuse herself by chasing rabbits, gophers, and chipmunks. When the cows were done grazing, they would lay down to chew their cud. I loved to snuggle up next to my favorite cow, Cherry, especially in cooler weather. And she seemed to enjoy the company, too. She would lay still, let me lie next to her, and sometimes blissfully fall asleep. However, when I was with Cherry or any of the cows, Trixie maintained her distance. Because she was part of the cow herding process, she was neither encouraged by me or accepted by Cherry or the other cows to come closer.

CHAPTER 4
THE TRIANGLE

One especially hot day just after I started the fourth grade, we were loading hay onto a wagon with a pitchfork. We were trying to get a load of hay into the barn before a storm. My grandfather Pojeta was helping, but he worked the horses too hard. The horses pulled the wagon into the barn and before we could unharness them, Babe dropped dead. My father replaced Babe with our first tractor, a steel-wheeled Farmall F-12. We kept Dolly, but she was only used to pull the cultivator in the garden. I remember the truck coming to pick up Babe. She was sold to a glue factory. Now instead of walking behind a team of horses I drove the tractor. I was nine years old.

✳ ✳ ✳ ✳ ✳ ✳

That autumn, we spent a lot of Saturdays and weekday evenings clearing trees and brush from a narrow strip of ground between two fields to install a fence to pasture cows. When the clearing was complete, a huge pile of brush and trees were set on fire. It was an intense blaze that reminded me of the horrible chicken house fire. After it burned, all that remained was a small pile of ashes. I was amazed and wondered, *Where did all that mass go?* It was all converted into heat and light energy. I remembered what we were taught in Religion class: "From dust thou art... to dust thou shall return." I thought, *What if dust is just an understandable term for that energy?*

I really did not know what energy was. I later learned that energy has different names depending on its interaction with matter: mechanical, thermal, electrical, nuclear, chemical, solar. Also, energy is neither created nor destroyed— it exists. I tried to understand what energy is. The best answer that I could come up with is that it is a phenomenon of nature or a fundamental property of nature. This has not satisfied my quest for the identification of energy. If everything comes from and goes back to energy, there must be a large amount of energy. Energy must be infinite. Accordingly, energy must be Supreme. If we come from energy, then we must be an image of the Supreme. That concept has stayed with me forever.

* * * * * *

At school, I was good at and liked math. In the fourth grade I also enjoyed religion class, especially preparing to become an altar boy. However, learning the Latin responses to the priest was a real struggle. I enjoyed serving at Mass, especially the time I served at a wedding because I was paid. However, since most weddings were on Saturdays and my father forced me to work all day on the farm, I never got the chance to do it again. During a religion class, a nun explained the mystery of the Holy Trinity— three persons in one God. I equated the Trinity to an equilateral triangle. That weekend I made an equilateral triangle out of wood about six inches high and painted it white. With a blue crayon I labeled the apexes "Father," "Son," and "Holy Ghost." In the center I wrote "God." I gave it to my teacher, and she used it in future classes as a visual aid.

* * * * * * *

Two life changing events occurred that year: first, my father began beating me. The beatings occurred frequently and continued over the next several years, until about the eighth grade. I have no memory of what caused the beatings with his belt, sticks, or the razor strap he used to sharpen tools. I remember my hair being pulled, being kicked. I remember being beat in the barn, in the fields, behind the garage. At the end of some of the beatings, he would kick me in the legs or my back and tell me that I was good for nothing and would never amount to anything. When he came home from work at midnight, he would get a gallon of his homemade wine and start drinking. My mother would always get up to feed him and listen to his complaining about the job. His complaints were very loud and would often wake me. There were times I was called downstairs just so he could beat me. One time my mother yelled for him to stop saying, "He's just a boy, he's just a boy!" She stepped between the two of us and he stopped. He never hit her. Another time we were behind the barn, he took off his belt and started lashing me severely. I begged him, "Please stop." I was on the ground and I looked up at him and saw in his eyes an indescribable fear, hatred, and rage. He stopped and kicked me several times in the torso. I laid there in tremendous pain. I never cried. I can't remember ever crying when he beat me.

My father would whip me like he whipped the horses when he demanded they pull harder at a load that was already taxing the team's maximum strength. Often I thought of running away, but I didn't know how to make it happen. Twice I discussed with my mother the idea of the family leaving my father. I tried to persuade her to leave the horror of our miserable lives on the farm. She said that she was trapped with nowhere to go and had to remain and endure the misery. Only a few years before, I had been his traveling companion searching for a farm and we were friends. I was never able to determine what caused the change.

Sometimes the nuns at school would look at my neck and hands. I thought they were checking to see if I was clean. They asked how I got the marks and bruises. I was too ashamed to tell and would say I didn't know or couldn't remember. No help or intervention ever came. Those beatings left me with lifelong physical, mental, and emotional scars.

My mother had a small holy water font attached to each door frame leading out of the house. When we would exit the house, we dipped our hands into the water and made the sign of the cross for safe passage outside. I thought if I drank some of it I might become a better boy and it would alleviate the beatings. I tried it many times with no success— the beatings kept coming. Over the next several years, he would beat me often, but I can't remember there ever being a reason. I searched for an explanation but could not find one. I wanted a better life. I wanted the beatings to stop. I had no memory of any of my sisters or brothers being treated this way. I was his whipping post.

* * * * * *

The second thing that happened was I developed a strong dislike for school and my grades went downhill. I was only allowed to do my homework on Sundays after Mass. I was promoted to fifth grade, but it was conditional. I would have been happy to drop out at that time. The effect of the agony I suffered in childhood made me realize that I had a father I could not depend on. I would have to become a self-made man.

Each summer, my grandpa Bartik would spend a weeklong vacation at the farm. He would bring his fishing gear. In the evening after all the chores were done, we would walk to a nearby lake hidden in the neighbor's woods. We would fish or try to catch fish. We talked till it started to get dark and we needed to return to the farm. Those weeks were wonderful times being with him. In the daytime, he would bring a book or newspaper and accompany me when I went to work in the fields. He was my confidant, my friend, my buddy, my hero. He was my one week a year Dad. At the end of his visit, I would beg him to stay longer rationalizing that since he was retired he didn't have to hurry back home. His response was wise. To this day I still remember and follow it: "You always leave when they still want you to stay." I loved my Gramps.

1951-1962

GROWING UP

CHAPTER 5
CHRISTMAS TIME

Christmases on the farm were a joyful time. We started preparing just after Thanksgiving. At night, my mother and the oldest children would bake. We would break black walnuts and take the meat and blend it into the dough for cookies. We made paper ornaments for the tree. About a week before Christmas, we would go out into the woods and cut down a pine tree, bring it home and put it on the back porch where it would stay until December 23. The tree cutting was a fun experience. Most every year there was a lot of snow. We would hitch the stone bolt (a flat sled without runners) to the horse or tractor. We would pick a tree and sometimes it was so big that we just cut the top off and used it. When we brought the tree into the house we put it in the stand and let the branches warm up and spread out.

The day of Christmas Eve was exciting. We woke up earlier than usual and did the morning chores of milking the cows, cleaning the barn stalls, and feeding the animals. But it didn't seem ordinary—we were filled with anticipation. After eating breakfast, I would begin decorating the tree. My mother and sisters would start preparing the evening dinner, which seemed like a feast. There were always lots of traditional Czechoslovakian pastries with peaches, pears, honey, and cinnamon. While the girls worked on the meal, I would put the lights on the tree and ensure they were working. They were the type of lights that if one bulb went out the whole string was bad. After the lights were on, the girls would hang the ornaments. We all had special ones we made like paper chains and strings of popcorn. The youngest Pojeta, who was not an infant, had the honor of placing the star or angel upon the top of the tree. In 1951, it was Judy.

We placed the gifts we made for one another next to the Nativity scene. My gifts were almost always made of wood such as a toy duck on a string and a potholder hanger shaped like a chef. We never put the wisemen with Mary and Joseph and Jesus. They were always off to the side on the bookshelf, because they were en route and wouldn't arrive until Epiphany. I would get a head start on the evening chores so that they could be done quickly and not disrupt the festivities.

* * * * * * *

The evening meal was wonderful. When we were almost done eating my mother or father would say they heard a noise and we better hide because Jesus was coming with our presents. They didn't believe in Santa Claus. We would all run into our parents' room and try to peek out the windows to see Jesus. After a while, my father would join us in the bedroom and we would hear more noise. Eventually we would all come out and our presents were under the tree. Our presents were usually clothes and things we needed and occasionally a toy. However, this Christmas would be very different. My father was unemployed due to a strike at the railroad. For several weeks before Christmas I knew things would be different in the presents department and we should not expect any gifts besides the ones we made.

During our meal, we heard a car horn and I ran to the window and saw a car leaving our property with its lights off. I could not determine the make or color of the car in the darkness. My father went outside to see who it was, as we were not expecting company. A minute later he came into the house carrying a large box. We gathered around and opened it. There were a lot of gifts for the girls like dolls and clothes. At the very bottom was a package with my name on it. I tore the paper and there it was: an electric O27 gauge Lionel train set with an engine, a tender, four freight cars, a caboose, and track to form an oval. I set the track up and enjoyed the train going around and around. We never found out who delivered those gifts. It was the greatest Christmas present of my entire childhood.

CHAPTER 6
MIDDLE AND HIGH SCHOOL

By the time I reached middle school age, I was assigned an additional farm task: beekeeper for our hives. We had four beehives which provided all the sweetness our family needed. I developed a love of the taste of honey which has never diminished my entire life. This task did not require a lot of time, but I was grateful for any chore that kept me from working the fields. My father taught me what needed to be done. I only wore head and face protection, but my father wore all the protective equipment possible. For some reason I could not fathom, bees would not sting me but constantly stung my father. I read books about beekeeping and talked to other beekeepers. I felt I knew more about bees than anyone else in my grade school. When I had to write a report in school, I wrote about bees and when I was required to give a presentation at school, I talked about bees. My dislike for school dissipated even though I struggled with the homework because I never had enough time. Math and science were my favorites and I excelled in both. My father acquired a second used tractor, a WC Allis-Chalmers. It was an electric start all rubber tricycle and much more powerful than the F-12. This meant we could do more farm work with two tractors in the field, father and son.

* * * * * *

I worked out a business deal with my father. I would buy a pair of rabbits, make a hutch for them, take care of, and feed them. When there was a litter, I would raise them to maturity to sell. I had to give half of the proceeds to my father. In no time at all, I was building multiple hutches and about two years later, I had so many rabbits that I put up a sign on the road that read "Rabbits for sale — live or dressed $1.00." There was a road crew doing resurfacing work and they bought all the rabbits dressed. I put my half of the proceeds in the bank in a savings account. Interestingly, when the rabbits would get loose, Trixie would catch them and hold them down with her paws for me, but she would never kill or eat my "business rabbits." Liquidating my rabbits netted enough of a profit to buy my first pair of sheep. When the lambs matured, I sold the rams and kept the ewes, and my herd increased. When I had over two dozen, I sold them at a livestock auction. I made enough money to purchase two bull calves. I raised the bull calves for beef and when I sold them, I purchased several more bull calves. This business cycle repeated all through high school in hopes to acquire enough money to pay for college. No matter what business venture I engaged in, I was required to give my father half of the proceeds. I found an old beat-up vacuum tube radio. The exterior was broken, but I could tune in a Chicago country music station which I really enjoyed. I put the radio in the barn to listen to while doing chores. I think the cows liked the music too because they seemed content.

* * * * * * *

When I was in the fifth grade, my entire class began preparing for the sacrament of Confirmation. We were required to memorize the Baltimore Catechism. Although it was a challenge, it was easier than memorizing the Latin responses required to be an altar boy. We knew that prior to the actual anointing the bishop would quiz us on our knowledge of the Catholic faith. We were told that if we did not answer correctly we would have to go to the back of the church and study more. Unlike Baptism, when I was an infant and could not choose my godparents, at Confirmation I was mature enough to choose a sponsor to guide me through the sacrament. I chose my hero, my grandfather, and took his name Albert as my Confirmation name. Back when I made my first Holy Communion, I was exempted from doing chores that day. I had hoped that set the precedent for Confirmation as well; however, that was not the case.

* * * * * *

In May of 1952, when I was 12 years old, God finally sent me some help with the farm work when my brother Robert was born. Soon after in September of 1953, I got a second brother, Richard. Unfortunately, I would leave the farm for college before they were any help at all. Rainy days were my favorite because we couldn't work in the fields. All our farm equipment was outdated and in disrepair which meant it frequently broke down. I would always accompany my father on trips to find replacement parts or someone to repair them. By the time I was in the eighth grade, I was responsible for equipment maintenance and repairs. Also, when I was in the 8th grade, I started driving myself and my little sisters to school on a special restricted farm use driver's license. Actually, I had been driving on the farm since about third grade. During recess at school, we played sandlot football and I really enjoyed it. I was very fast and agile; I was frequently given the ball and almost always scored.

* * * * * *

The summer my sister Mary was two years old, she liked playing on a little scooter in the path leading to the fields that ran between the garage and the garden. This portion of the path contained a large quantity of sand that she used as a huge sandbox. One day, my father was driving the Allis-Chalmers tractor pulling me on a hay rake. He decided to stop alongside the garage to grease the hay rake. When he was done, he drove the tractor into Mary's sandbox. He heard a strange noise and stopped. He had run over Mary. Her body was under the tractor and her head was squeezed between the two front tires. She was alive and crying as he pulled her out. At the time, my mother was sick in bed with a migraine headache so I held Mary as my father drove to the Emergency Room. She was examined and x-rayed, and other than some bruises, she was unharmed and we took her home.

* * * * * *

In the fall of 1954, I started high school at Saint Joseph's. It was a brand-new school across from the golf course from Notre Dame University in South Bend, Indiana. It was 25 miles from our house. I drove my sisters to Saint Mary's and caught a free bus to the high school to save on gas. The summer before the school year started, I had signed up for the freshman football team. The first week, we practiced in the mornings and I would drive there and be home by noon still able to work a full day on the farm till dark. I dreamed of being the quarterback. Starting the second week, afternoon practices were added. My father forced me to drop out as my labor was required on the farm. I was so very disappointed. I was never allowed to do any activities outside of school. I wanted to join 4-H and the Boy Scouts, but my father forbid me from doing anything that would cut into my working on the farm.

I took college prep classes in high school and it was much more demanding than my grade school curriculum. My father believed that except for doing the necessary chores, Sunday was a day of rest. Therefore, this was my only time during the week to do my schoolwork. I worked out arrangements with my teachers to get all the requirements for the next week and did it all day on Sundays after Mass. When the weather permitted, I would take my books and my trusted companion, Trixie, to my favorite spot: a huge flat rock under a shade tree. The rock served as my desk. I had a job in high school to work off half of the $100 tuition each year. After school, I would the clean a classroom: empty the trash, sweep the floors, wash the blackboards, and "bang" the erasers. After that, I would take the bus back to Saint Mary's and pick up my sisters who would be waiting for me because their school day was shorter than mine. By the time I got home, my father had already left for his night job and it was my responsibility to do all the evening chores.

* * * * * * *

I really enjoyed high school. After eight years of female teachers, nuns from the Sisters of Saint Joseph, I finally had male teachers, Brothers from the University of Notre Dame Order of the Holy Cross. Even though I struggled keeping up with my course work, I still managed to do extra credit projects such as making a scale model of Shakespeare's Globe Theater for my junior year literature class. I recreated the stage with a trap door and staging mechanisms. My mother helped by sewing the curtains. It was extremely difficult to get physical measurements and facts about the structure in the pre-internet world. My teacher was very helpful in assisting me with research. We found an article with sketches of the structure and people standing next to it. I assumed the height of a man to be 5'10" to calculate the dimensions. My model remained on display in my high school's trophy showcase for decades after I graduated as reported by my youngest siblings.

* * * * * * *

My grades in high school were very good, almost straight As, despite my challenges and time constraints. I began thinking that academics could be my ticket off the farm. The physical beatings ceased as I grew bigger and stronger, but the mental and emotional abuse persisted. My father screamed at me and constantly criticized me. I never received a single compliment from him. I had no relationship with my father. I could not talk to him about anything without being verbally abused. This left a huge void in my life. I felt inferior and ashamed when school buddies talked about things they did with their dads. I did have a closer and loving relationship with my mother. I could talk to her and I felt she understood me. I explained to her that as soon as I graduated from high school, I was leaving the farm. My first choice would be to attend college and study mechanical engineering. If that didn't work out for whatever reason, financial or otherwise, I would enter a vocational school to study tool and die design/making. If both of those were not possible, I was going to enlist in the military. I could see sadness in her eyes as I explained this to her. She loved her children and couldn't bear to lose one of them. However, I believe she fully understood and appreciated the situation that I was in.

CHAPTER 7
DISASTERS

January 1957, halfway through my junior year in high school, was a brutally cold and snowy month. One Sunday evening, my father decided to pull the car into the barn so that it would be easier to start on Monday morning. However, the car would not start and he thought it was due to frozen water in the gas line. His plan was to use a blow torch to thaw it. After filling the blow torch with gasoline, he brought it into the kitchen to preheat it. He stuck a match and the blow torch exploded, spewing gasoline throughout the entire kitchen and all over himself. In an instant, the kitchen was an inferno; the walls and curtains were ablaze. My mother yelled for all of us children to get out of the house. My father was badly burned but continued to try to put the fire out. We had no telephone and all I could think to do was to go for help. I ran across several fields in knee deep snow the two miles to the Hanes' house, the nearest farm that had a phone, and called the volunteer fire department. The firemen were already at the house by the time I walked back home.

Both floors of the entire north side of the house were engulfed in flames and windows were exploding. The fire chief had already radioed the next town, Edwardsburg, for help. I overheard the fire chief tell my father they were running out of water, and even with the arrival of another unit, he didn't think they could save the house. My father asked if they had a water pump on the truck. They did. My father told him that we had a pond across the road and ordered me to go chop a hole in the ice. A volunteer firefighter followed me with the portable pump. The ice was at least a foot thick and when I chopped through it I hit gravel. I moved father onto the pond and started chopping a second hole while the firefighter went for more hose. Finally, I struck water as the Edwardsburg fire department arrived on the scene and the two units got the blaze under control. When the fire was out, about a quarter of the house was destroyed: the kitchen and an upstairs room that held all our clothes. I was so exhausted from running and chopping that I went into the barn and laid down on the hay to rest. That night, one of our neighbors took all ten of us into their home and we stayed there for several weeks until our house was habitable again. That added hours of work to my days as we had to travel back and forth to do the morning and evening chores and care for the animals. We missed school on Monday, but we were back in class on Tuesday. The insurance did not cover the repairs and it created even more financial hardship.

* * * * * * *

In my four years of high school, l l was only allowed to attend one football game and two dances. The morning after my junior prom, my father woke me at 6 am to gas up the tractor and start disking to prepare the soil for planting corn. I was half asleep. I went to start the F-12 tractor, but forgot to retard the spark and pushed down on the crank and it backfired. I was picked up from the ground and thrown 10 feet from the tractor. Looking down at my right wrist, I could see two bones poking through my skin. My father came over and decided he would "fix" my wrist. He pulled my hand to try and straighten the bone. I was in excruciating pain. I stood and held my wrist with my left hand and walked to the back porch. My mother came out and I passed out in her arms. After coming to, they took me to the hospital where my arm was put in a cast and I was admitted. It was three days of beautiful rest and plentiful food. Life in the hospital— away from the farm— was good. I returned to school in time for finals and tried to make the most of my injury stating I could not write and asked to be exempted from taking finals. However, the Brothers weren't buying it and told me to do the best I could with my left hand.

* * * * * * *

The two dances I attended were my junior and senior proms. Both times, I escorted a very nice and pretty girl named Mary Ann. In fact, she was a beauty queen, Miss Cassopolis. She was the youngest daughter of friends of my parents. Outside of the two proms, we never dated. However, she always accompanied her parents when they came to visit mine. The rumor was that when boys came to pick Mary Ann up for dates, they were greeted by her father and introduced to his baseball bat and told that if she was harmed, he would break the bat across their heads. I was never introduced to the bat; I think her parents liked me. I liked Mary Ann very much, but I was motivated to attend college and earn a degree in mechanical engineering. I made a promise to myself that after graduation from college, I would work for at least two years as an engineer before getting seriously involved with a girl. After high school graduation, Mary Ann and I lost track of each other. I later learned from my sister Dorothy that she married a law student from Notre Dame.

* * * * * * *

In my physics class, we discussed the generation of electricity by the means of an electro-static generator. Since it appeared that with some modifications I could gather all the necessary items from junk lying around the farm, I decided to build one. Fabrication of my electro-static generator went smoothly, but the time came to check out its functionality. There was a small challenge, I didn't have the instrumentation to measure the electrical output. However, I did have a young brother, Bob, who was always interested in what I was doing and willing to get involved. All I had to do was invite him to hold two wires. Bob was suspicious that it might inflict discomfort or pain and initially refused. My next approach was to offer him money— a nickel. He still refused so I upped the ante and assured him that if he were injured I would give a dime, but he would get the nickel regardless of the outcome. Bob knew how thrifty I was with my money and finally accepted the offer.

Bob cautiously held the wires. I turned the crank, and he let out a shrill scream. My mother came rushing up to my room to see who was hurt. Since my bedroom was my amateur experimental test laboratory, my mother was used to frequent noises and smoke. In fact, my parents would not leave me home alone and always ensured one of my sisters 'babysat' me to prevent destruction of the house. I received a scolding about trying to electrocute my five-year-old brother. I tried to minimize my culpability by telling my mom I just needed someone to hold the wires, but she wasn't buying it. I paid Bob the full fifteen cents. It was worth it to prove my machine worked.

CHAPTER 8
EMPLOYMENT

A few days before the end of my junior year, a classmate and buddy of mine told me he was quitting his floor sweeper job at Bertram Products Incorporated and they might be hiring a replacement. The first Sunday of summer vacation, I removed my cast with a pair of tin snips even though it had been on for less than a month. On Monday, I went to Bertram Products. It was a small job shop that employed about 20 people on two shifts. They subcontracted and made small parts for Studebaker automobiles and Bendix Aerospace Corporation. I filled out an application and was interviewed by the owner and he hired me on the spot to start working the next day. The pay was $1.00 an hour. I asked to start the following Monday because I knew my hand was still injured and I wanted to have a little longer for it to heal.

I worked 40 hours a week, Monday through Friday, from 7:30 am to 4:30 pm. My father agreed to it because I could still do all the morning and evening chores and farm as there was plenty of daylight. However, he demanded I turn my entire paycheck over to him. My mother gave me $5.00 a week for spending money. I didn't mind the factory work. It was better than the farm. I was a good hard worker and did whatever was asked of me. It was a non-union shop. I swept floors, moved trays of parts between machines for the machinists to perform their functions, and delivered and picked up parts that needed to be cadmium-plated by another factory.

I soon became the go-to guy when a machinist, foreman, or the owner needed something done. In fact, the owner once had me go to his home and set forms for his concrete driveway to be poured. After working there a month, I approached the owner and asked him how long an employee had to work there before being entitled to a raise. My next paycheck included a 10%, one dime, an hour raise. I worked that entire summer. When school started, they asked me to stay on two nights a week and Saturdays. I still had to do all the morning chores, but my sisters pitched in and did the evening chores on those nights. When I turned eighteen, I immediately became a machinist running a lathe, drill press, and milling machine at $1.50 an hour. I stayed in that job until I resigned to go to college. The owner wanted me to stay on and offered me a job when I came home for the holidays and summer vacations during college. My father continued to allow the arrangement because I brought in a lot of much needed money for the family. My mother wrote me a letter and told me that she saved all the money I made the last summer and would give it to me when I left for college.

* * * * * * *

I started my senior year of high school in the fall of 1957. Because St. Joe's was a college prep school, all my classmates and I could talk about was where we would go to college and what we were going to study. I wanted to study engineering. My excitement overflowed and I started to talk about college plans at home with my parents. My father made it clear that he planned for me to attend Norte Dame University and live at home so I could continue to work on the farm. I reconciled myself to my fate, even though I desperately wanted to leave the farm after high school. One day after a parent-teacher conference, my counselor, Brother James, asked me to come to his office. He told me he had a serious discussion with my father and explained that even though I was a bright student, I would never be able to work full time on the farm and keep up with the rigors of an engineering degree program.

Brother James suggested I consider an alternate college, a Catholic school with a highly regarded engineering program, Marquette University in Milwaukee, Wisconsin. For several days I pondered how to present this alternative to my parents. Eventually, my father told me I should apply to another Catholic college in addition to Notre Dame in case I wasn't accepted. It seemed that Brother James convinced him, but my father made it seem like it was his idea. I applied to both schools and was accepted by both. Although I would have loved to go to Notre Dame, I knew it would not be in my best interest.

That year, I was required to register with Selective Service for the draft. I did, but also applied for a student deferment. My fear was that my education would be interrupted and I would not earn my engineering degree that I so desperately longed for. My draft board had no problem achieving their quota and granted me a 2-S student deferment. Now all the pieces of the puzzle were falling into place.

* * * * * * *

Tom at his high school graduation

During high school, I became increasingly aware of racial conflicts in the South. I heard my elders and classmates discuss news reports of killings, bombings, and desegregation of schools. There were so many bombings in Birmingham, Alabama, that it was referred to as "Bombingham." I never fully understood the situation for two reasons. First, I was occupied with farm and schoolwork. I felt I needed to get the best grades possible as it was my ticket off the farm. Secondly, my life experience with race relations did not include conflict.

We lived about three miles from a black farmer named Romy whose sons were part of a team of men and boys who went from farm to farm to help bring in the harvest. Black and white men worked side by side in the fields, while black and white women worked side by side in the kitchens to feed them. It was hard work, but also a social occasion. The women seemed to compete for the compliment of best food each year. Romy was very old. I remember him telling my father stories of his life as a slave in Alabama. He was an accomplished stonecutter. His sons would haul rocks they cleared from the fields, he cut them, and his sons built the house. When the house was finished and his family moved in, Romy invited my parents and me to the housewarming party. I still remember that house. It was very nice, so much nicer than our house. Most of my classmates at school were white, there were only a few black students each year. The only difference I was ever able to discern was the colors of our skin. I could not comprehend the turmoil in the South.

Over the decade since we moved from the city to the farm, I had learned to hate and despise my existence. I had been trapped and could not leave, although at least twice during high school I again seriously considered running away. Life was harsh. I was prevented from partaking in normal activities that I saw others my age enjoying. However, those ten years were the crucible that defined who I am. I fear if conditions had been different, I would be a different person. Despite all the baggage my childhood produced, and I was burdened to carry, I am very satisfied with who I am. I did the very best I could with all the talents God had blessed me with.

CHAPTER 9
OFF TO COLLEGE

In August 1958, the day I departed for college began like any other. I did the morning chores and ate breakfast. The car had been packed the night before with my belongings— all my books and clothes. I said goodbye to my tearful sisters and my faithful companion Trixie who I would thoroughly miss. My parents drove me to Milwaukee. I never lived on the farm again, I only returned for short visits. I never stayed longer than five days— the amount of time my father and I could tolerate one another before the tension between us reached a boiling point. My deep sadness was that I could not take my best friend and companion, my beloved Trixie, with me. Although I physically left the farm behind, the emotional scars would be with me for the rest of my life and I would have to learn to live with the pain.

My parents helped me unload my things into my dormitory room on the second floor of Nicholas Hall. They needed to depart immediately to get back to the farm for evening chores. Several hours later, my roommate John and his mother arrived. We agreed on which desk and bed we each would use. Once his mother departed, we began to get acquainted. Luckily, we were both engineering students. John told me of his high school achievements, including winning a science competition for developing a rocket. He casually mentioned his IQ was 176, and all I could think was, "How am I ever going to compete?"

* * * * * *

The next day after orientation and getting my schedule and textbooks I met the dorm house mother, Mrs. Callahan. I told her I was searching for work and she offered me a part-time job as a desk monitor. The job was to answer the phone on evenings and weekends and to lock the doors at curfew. I would share a dorm room with the other desk monitor, Carl. The engineering program was on a quarter system and had already started. Carl was a junior in the speech program which was on the semester system and he would arrive in September. The salary was a free room. I was thrilled to be offered the job because it would stretch my budget. I knew I only had sufficient resources to fund my freshman year. I accepted the job and was reassigned to a smaller room on the first floor next to the lobby telephone and door.

My new next-door neighbor was Father MacEvoy, a rotund Jesuit priest, the dorm chaplain. He was also a religion teacher and the chaplain of the dental school. His nickname was the "Wisconsin Avenue Apostle" and his claim to fame was the numerous people he had converted to Catholicism. He had served as a Jesuit chaplain in World War II. The evening I met him, he made it clear to me that no matter the time, day or night, if anyone came to see him, I was to unlock the door and let them in. He became my confessor, my mentor, and my friend. He was also responsible for getting me many jobs during my college days including cashier at the dental school cafeteria and shoveling snow at the girls' dormitories.

Father Mac had a nickname for everybody. My nickname was "Clarence." I suspected I was named for the innocent "wingless" Angel from *It's a Wonderful Life.* Several of my dormmates agreed that I looked like a Clarence. I am still waiting for a little bell to ring so that I may receive my wings. Father Mac was on a mission to get me to become a Jesuit priest. He had a friend named Father Jerome who would visit frequently. If Father Mac wasn't there, Father Jerome would strike up conversations and called me "Leonardo DaVinci."

* * * * * *

One Saturday morning when I was on duty, Father Jerome stopped by and we started talking about the existence of God and how to prove it. He said: "Pick anything. Where did it come from?" I said: "My parents." He said: "Where did they come from?" I said: "My grandparents." And he said: "What caused them?" Eventually we were back to the cavemen. This led us to discuss evolution and the sea— and the 'Big Bang.' Finally, he asked, "Who caused the Big Bang?" He loved to discuss— and prove— the existence of God through cause-and-effect statements. This always led to the "Uncaused Cause"— that which was not caused by anything, it just is. The Uncaused Cause is God or God is the Uncaused Cause. If energy is infinite, then energy and the Uncaused Cause are one in the same. I felt I could repaint my grade school triangle and replace "God the Father" with "Energy." Many years later I read Saint Thomas Aquinas' *Summa Theologica*. He wrote in excruciating detail (but used the same logic as Father Jerome did with me) about the argument for the existence of God. Aquinas also repeatedly tried to prove the non-existence of God but was unsuccessful.

* * * * * * *

My roommate Carl arrived. He was a black man from Memphis, Tennessee. His father was a Lutheran minister. We had a cordial roommate relationship, but we never became friends. Carl only socialized with other upperclassmen black students. Most of the young men in the dorm were freshmen. Everyone had an open-door policy and we would pop into each other's rooms to study or socialize. If a door was closed, the practice was to knock first. I noticed a trend that confused and upset me. When boys from the South would come to my dorm room, they always asked if Carl was there. If he was, they would not come in. If Carl wasn't in the room, they would enter and hang out. I learned that the southern boys had a very different attitude towards blacks than I did. Suddenly, all the talk about race relations I had heard in my youth started to make sense.

* * * * * * *

I worked very hard and got all As and Bs. It seemed to me that I had to work harder than others for my good grades. I was never tested (and never wanted to know) my IQ, but I attributed my scholastic success to the work ethic drilled into me on the farm. My "one-day" roommate John failed out of the engineering program. He struggled with the course load and often came to me for help. I probably spent too much time helping him. At the end of the second quarter, he was called to the Dean's office and invited to leave. He eventually returned and attended the law school successfully. Unlike high school, in college I went to many football games and dances. I dated many girls, but never the same one more than twice. My priority was to earn my degree, work for at least two years, and be debt-free before a romantic involvement.

* * * * * *

After freshman year, I did not return to the farm. Instead, I rented a room and took a full-time job as a machine cleaner on the third shift at Milwaukee Continental Can Company. They made beer and vegetable cans. I also carried six credit hours of classes that summer. In my sophomore year, the College of Engineering changed from a quarter system to a semester system. This allowed Engineering students to take additional courses in the other colleges. Because I was still concerned about the financial feasibility of finishing my degree, I got special permission to take 20 credit hours a semester. I gave up my dorm job and was hired by Marquette High School as a waiter in the faculty dining facility in exchange for room and board.

* * * * * *

My sophomore year I shared a dorm room with three other guys. Two of them had their own bedrooms and I shared a bedroom with Leroy Taegar. Leroy was a bi-racial pre-med student from British Honduras (present-day Belize). We talked about our lives and shared our hopes and dreams. He was five years older than me. Like me, he was from a very poor family and graduated from a Jesuit Catholic high school. He always encouraged me to come visit him in his country. He said his family would welcome me. He asked me to call him "Sess" which was his nickname back home. I knew I would never be able to invite him to my family's farm because I would be embarrassed by our poverty. He was a very gifted student and loved to play soccer. His high school and government awarded him a full scholarship for college and medical school with the promise that he would return to his country to practice medicine. After our sophomore year, we went on to different living arrangements, but occasionally we would run into one another on campus.

* * * * * *

In December 1959, I received a letter from my mother with the birth announcement of the ninth Pojeta child, my baby sister, Catherine (Cathy). I met her on my Christmas vacation. A short time later she was diagnosed with Downs Syndrome. She grew to be a very loving child and a devoted companion to my parents until their deaths. At my mother's death, my sister Mary became Cathy's guardian.

* * * * * *

During my junior year, I joined the Ice-Skating Club. Also, I met a girl named Mary Ellen and we became the best of platonic friends. She was a commuter student studying to become a teacher. We came from totally different backgrounds. She lived in an upscale suburb of Milwaukee and was an only child. Her parents doted on her and she was the light of their lives. I spent much of my free time with her. Sometimes I took a bus to her house and sometimes her parents would let us use the family car, a Buick Roadmaster, and she would pick me up at the dorm. Our dates were always simple low-cost events. Her parents frequently invited me to Sunday dinner. However, I just was not ready for a serious relationship. After graduation, we never saw each other again. Every now and then I still think about her and hope everything in her life turned out well.

* * * * * * *

Mary Ellen and I were part of a social group of eight students who hung out at the student union. After the end of the 1961 football season, Marquette leadership announced that the university was discontinuing the football program to concentrate on academic excellence. The academic excellence focus didn't bother me. However, dropping football was disappointing. The following Monday while having my coffee and breakfast at the student union with my friends, I expressed my disapproval of the football decision. The discussion continued and soon a large group of students gathered around me agreeing with my viewpoint. I suggested that as loyal students at Marquette University, we needed to show our disapproval in the form of a student protest. My suggestion was met with enthusiastic verbal agreement. I led the group on a march through the campus to the administration building. As we marched we chanted: "We want football!" The group continued to grow to hundreds of students. After we passed the administrative offices someone asked, "Where to next?" All I could think to say was, "Let's go to City Hall." Now the crowd was over a thousand and we were disrupting traffic as we moved along and loudly chanted. By that time, reporters from the *Milwaukee Sentinel* newspaper arrived and were taking photographs. As we passed City

Hall, two students approached me and suggested we overturn a parked car. I told them that was out of the question, we were engaged in a peaceful protest. They accepted that decision and I felt I was the leader of the march and in control of the group.

I was wearing a trench coat carrying my books and slide rule for my first class (which I had skipped) under my arm. My slide rule had my name on it (Pojeta, Thos, Sr.) and the "Thos, Sr." part of it was visible to the news media. After leaving City Hall, we marched back to the administration building and continued our chant. We were greeted by several faculty members, including the Prefect of Discipline, Father Stemper. He approached me and requested I surrender my student ID and I gave it to him. Suddenly I had an alarming moment of clarity. I thought, *Oh my God, what is going to happen to me?* I was in my third year of college struggling to earn a degree, and I wanted to crawl in that little doghouse from my childhood and seek sanctuary.

I pulled away from the crowd and went back to the dorm where I ran into Father MacEvoy. He said he hoped I wasn't with those crazy kids out there and I told him what I had done. He uttered his famous line of disapproval, "You Pothead!" He ordered me to my room and told me to stay there. Later that evening, after dinner, he came to my room and handed me my student ID that he had retrieved from Father Stemper. The protest was on the national evening news and there were pictures in the newspapers. When I went home to the farm for Christmas, my sisters wanted to know if I knew the guy who led the protest: Thos Sr! When I told them it was me, they thought I was pretty cool.

* * * * * *

In the second semester of my junior year, I took a Machine Design course. The professor, Dr. Sadovy, announced he was searching for a student to do technical illustrations for the revision of his Machine Design chapter in *Marks Mechanical Engineering Handbook*. After class, I followed him to his office and told him I had taken a Mechanical Drafting class in high school and would like the opportunity to be his illustrator. There was another student who was also interested. He gave both of us an audition and I received the job. Dr. Sadovy fled Germany with his wife and children during World War II. He had a custom of mentoring students with financial need to get through school. He frequently invited me to his home for Sunday dinner with his wife and teenaged son and daughter. The children were fluent in English, but his wife could not speak English at all. I felt sorry for her because she must have felt isolated with only her family to talk to. I worked on the illustrations for several months and received a dollar an hour compensation. The illustrations were blueprints and had to be drawn in ink on mylar. Each illustration had to be done multiple times because of modifications. Dr. Sadovy and I developed a professional friendship that I hoped to continue after graduation. However, shortly after I graduated, he accepted a position as the dean of an engineering school in Munich.

CHAPTER 10
SENIOR YEAR

After three and a half years of college I had earned enough credit hours to graduate. However, I had taken one semester of a yearlong 8 credit hour course on Nuclear Reactor Design and I wanted to take the second half. Additionally, I was considering continuing my education in a master's program so, I enrolled in three graduate courses. One of the classes was Advanced Calculus which proved to be very challenging. It consisted mainly of proving that various mathematical relationships were continuous to infinity. It was difficult, but I learned that they could be proved to infinity plus x. During that course, strange as it sounds, infinity did not seem that large because there was something larger than infinity.

* * * * * * *

Because I was enrolled in the Nuclear Reactor Design course, I was invited to spend a week at Argon National Laboratory in Illinois. The purpose of the trip was to learn how to operate a nuclear sub-critical reactor and the fabrication of the nuclear control and fuel rods. For the Engineering Open House that last semester, my Academic Advisor asked me to demonstrate the functionality of a simulated nuclear reactor on an analog computer. I accepted, but thought a more interesting presentation would be the functionality of the suspension system of an automobile. Therefore, I did both. The car demonstration included simulating various sized vehicles, shock absorbers, springs, and bumps in the road. As I predicted, the visitors enjoyed watching the car bounce more than the nuclear reactor core functionality.

* * * * * *

Father McEvoy had arranged for six of us students to live in the basement of the dental school. We received room and board in exchange for working in the dental school cafeteria. I was the only engineering student and we all lived in one big room. There were lights, but no windows. Because it was crowded, I usually went to the cafeteria or library to study. We got to use the dental school faculty toilet and shower facilities, but only at odd hours. We served breakfast and lunch for the students and served at special dining events for fraternities and sororities.

* * * * * *

Though I was considering going right into a master's program, I decided to test the employment waters too. I applied to eight different companies and all of them came to campus to interview me. I was invited to six on-site visits and received seven job offers, all of which paid a salary that was more than twice as much as my father's income. I narrowed my choice to two companies: Babcock & Wilcox and McDonnell Aircraft. Both were in the middle of the seven salary offers, but one paid $5.00 a week more than the other.

I was very interested in the prospect of working at Babcock & Wilcox's nuclear reactor research site in Savannah, Georgia. They were developing nuclear sites such as Three Mile Island and nuclear submarine capabilities. I traveled to Akron, Ohio for the meeting. Their offer was a one-year orientation of all aspects of the company and then they would place me where they needed me. I liked the idea of the orientation and requested some assurance that I would be assigned to nuclear research. They were very interested in me; they called me three times and sent a recruiter to Marquette to meet with me twice. However, they wouldn't guarantee a place in nuclear research.

* * * * * * *

I interviewed with McDonnell Aircraft on campus. They explained their involvement in the Mercury and Gemini Space programs and the F-4 Phantom Fighter Jet, the fastest aircraft in the world at that time. The performance of the F-4 was classified "Secret." I would be working as a Test Engineer in the systems lab. They made me an offer and I requested a site visit. The recruiter told me they were not funding site visits, but I was welcome to tour the plant at my expense. I felt it was worth the investment to visit the company and meet the employees before I decided to accept or reject their offer.

I contacted their Human Resources office and scheduled a trip around my class schedule. I packed my only suit and took a train from Milwaukee to St. Louis. I arrived late in the afternoon and checked into a hotel near the facility. The following morning a Human Resources Officer met me for breakfast at the hotel and transported me to his office. Much to my delight they asked me to fill out a voucher for reimbursement of my travel expenses. I felt we were off to a good start! The engineer I would be working for escorted me to what would be my workspace on the second floor of building 103. There was an interior window with a view of the laboratory test facility where a 30-foot diameter chamber for Gemini astronaut altitude testing was under construction. My future boss showed me the desk and drafting table where I would work.

After returning to Marquette, I wrote thank you letters rejecting all the offers I received except Babcock & Wilcox and McDonnell Aircraft. I had another telephone conversation with Babcock & Wilcox and they reiterated they could not guarantee a position in nuclear research, so my decision was made. I accepted McDonnell's offer. I sent Babcock & Wilcox a cordial letter thanking them for their hospitality and declined their offer. Two days later I received a phone call from their Human Resources officer stating he just happened to be passing through Milwaukee and would like to take me to dinner the next day. I never felt so wanted.

I graciously accepted his offer as I had never heard of a college student turning down a free meal. He took me to a steakhouse and asked me what Babcock & Wilcox needed to do to get me to change my mind. He wanted to know if the salary offered was the issue. I assured him it wasn't about money; I just wanted a guarantee that after the year of orientation I could work in nuclear research. He reiterated the company's position and we parted on congenial terms. I was satisfied with my choice, and as a bonus, I would be able to continue my education on a part-time basis at McDonnell's expense. After I accepted the job, I ran into my old roommate

Leroy Taegar. I told him I was moving to St. Louis after graduation and extended an invitation to come and stay. I was pleased that I would finally have a place that I could invite people to visit. He told me he could never do that because he was biracial, and he had heard St. Louis was a clannish and racially divided town.

College was one of the best experiences of my life. I worked hard, never asking my parents for financial assistance and graduated debt-free. I met wonderful people and achieved my lifelong dream of earning an engineering degree. I had never experienced travel before I visited the companies that were trying to recruit me. My faith increased and relationship with God grew. I was introduced to Saint Jude, the Patron Saint of Hopeless Causes, and began my lifelong devotion to him.

Tom as a college senior

1962-1974
SPACE AND MARRIAGE

CHAPTER 11
FIRST ENGINEERING POSITION

Graduation Day finally arrived. My sister Dorothy wanted to buy me a class ring. I thanked her for her kind offer but told her since I did everything myself, I wanted to purchase my ring, too. My parents attended the graduation ceremony and immediately after, we packed all my books and belongings and drove back to the farm. A couple of days later, my father took me to a used car lot and I purchased my first car, a 1958 AMC Rambler American, with the money I had saved from jobs I did while in college. I was on top of the world. I was debt-free, owned a car, and had a degree in Engineering.

The next day, I decided to drive back to Milwaukee to say goodbye to my friends that I had not seen as our departure after graduation was so hasty. I stayed in Milwaukee for three days then returned to the farm. I packed everything I owned. My father gave me a screwdriver, a pair of pliers, and a box wrench that he said would come in handy if my car broke down. Before I departed, my father made it clear in no uncertain terms that he expected me to send part of my income home for tuition for my sisters to go to college. I sent money home every payday to help my father support his family. I left the farm on a Thursday at 9 pm and arrived in St. Louis at McDonnell Aircraft at 8 am on Friday morning. I spent the morning filling out paperwork and got a list of rooms to rent and a map. I was to start work on Monday morning. I set out to find a place to live.

* * * * * *

The first room on the list was two miles from work. The landlady was Mrs. Christine. It was a two-bedroom home. She and her daughter lived in the basement, and she rented the bedrooms for ten dollars a week. My room had a single bed, dresser, desk and chair, and a closet. Everyone in the home shared the one bathroom. I told Mrs. Christine I was interested but wanted to check out some of the other properties before deciding. I started for the next address and got stuck in Friday rush-hour traffic and got lost. I never did see another possible room, but eventually I found my way back to Mrs. Christine's house. I paid her a week's rent in advance and moved in. I was exhausted. I wrote a short letter to my parents to let them know my address and that I was alright.

Since I didn't know anyone, I spent Saturday alone. On Sunday, I found the closest Catholic church, Saint William's, and attended Mass. After Mass, I met the neighbor boy. He was a high school sophomore named Jimmy. He had suffered a birth injury and had difficulty walking. When Jimmy was a little boy, he rode around all the time with his father who was a cab driver. Consequently, he knew the area like the back of his hand. We developed a friendship and he helped me navigate my new hometown.

On Monday morning, I drove to work and checked in at the personnel office and got my badge so that I could clock in and out. I was an Associate Engineer. I met my supervisor, the Group Engineer, who had interviewed me, and he escorted me to my desk. He congratulated me and wished me well. He told me McDonnell was a good company to work for. However, that was his last week. He resigned and took another job. He introduced me to another engineer I would be working with, Bill, who gave me an orientation tour. My first assignment was to draw experimental mechanics plans for the test set up needed to determine the capabilities of a heat exchanger for the Gemini spacecraft.

* * * * * * *

After McDonnell Systems Engineers designed a component, it would come to us Test Engineers. We conducted tests to evaluate the performance of a new design or modifications to hardware and systems. We also analyzed failures and addressed safety concerns. The Systems Engineer responsible for a particular aspect of the Gemini spacecraft would write a request for a test. My section would receive the request and cost it out: determine the engineering, technician, and mechanic man-hours, as well as the cost of special instrumentation or hardware. That cost estimate would be reviewed by management for approval and returned to the requester who would approve the program, establish a budget, and set up a schedule. During all phases of testing, there was constant communication with the requester regarding the status and results of the project. Upon completion, a report was drafted by the Test Engineer and submitted for approval.

* * * * * * *

During lunch one afternoon with other new hires (another male engineer and two single female mathematicians), we discussed going on a picnic to a nearby man-made lake just outside St. Louis the following Sunday. After Mass, I drove out to the lake and met up with the others. It was a beautiful sunny day and very crowded. We were having a pleasant time watching young people swimming and jumping off a raft. One of the ladies, Maureen, asked me to swim out to the raft with her. I was a very poor swimmer, but I figured I could make the short distance. About half-way to the raft, I developed cramps in my legs. I began to struggle and panic. I went under and swallowed a lot of water. When I surfaced, I was thrashing around and Maureen couldn't offer much help. I went down a second time. When I resurfaced, I tried to grab hold of something. I feared I would drown. My only thought was that I had just been to Mass and received Holy Communion. I was at peace with whatever might happen. I went under again and everything went black. The next thing I remembered was several people trying to pull me into a boat. A lifeguard brought me back to shore in the boat. I laid on the beach resting and embarrassed beyond words. At the end of the day, I drove home. I was happy to be alive and guessed God still had plans for me.

* * * * * * *

I continued working under the mentorship of Bill for several weeks. With each test, he increased my responsibilities. One day there was a request to verify the performance of a gas ejection system on the F-4 Phantom Fighter and he said, "It's yours." The F-4 Phantom had an internally mounted 20mm multi-barrel gun in the turret. When it fired, it emitted a large quantity of gun smoke. Under most flight conditions, it did not affect the functionality of the aircraft. However, the F-4 pilots in Vietnam discovered that under a specific angular bank maneuver, the discharged gun smoke would extinguish the jet engine. By performing a correcting maneuver, pilots had been able to restart the engine without mishap so far, but it was still unacceptable. Therefore, the F-4 system designers devised a gas ejection system to correct the issue and it needed to be tested for safety, structural integrity, and airworthiness— and that was my assignment. Management approved my plans and the test was authorized. It didn't feel like work. It was fun and I enjoyed myself. I would arrive early and have my breakfast in the cafeteria before work. I would depart around 6 pm and go back to my room to check if I received any mail. Then I would grab dinner at a local burger joint and head back to work for a few more hours. I didn't know anyone except the people at work. Rather than sit around my room, I would go in on Saturdays as well. About the time I completed the report, I received my Secret Clearance and my Critical Skill Deferment from the draft board in Michigan. I would not be drafted to go to Vietnam.

* * * * * * *

About two months into my new job, my father called on a Monday morning to tell me that my grandfather Bartik had died the day before. He was my favorite, my one-week-a year Dad during my farm days. He was my mentor and buddy. I chose him to be my Confirmation sponsor and took his name, Albert, at my Confirmation. He was my hero. He was my "Gramps." I was saddened that he passed away before I had a chance to share my experiences as an engineer with him. I received permission to take an advance of my vacation time, five days, to attend his funeral in Chicago.

CHAPTER 12
GATEWAY TO THE WEST ARCH

Shortly after arriving in St. Louis, I learned construction of the Arch was underway and it sparked my interest. The Gateway Arch was going to be an inverted catenary, 630 feet high, 630 feet wide at the base between its two legs. It was to be constructed with 54 stainless steel triangular sections. It would include a transport system in the center of each leg leading to a 65-foot by 7-foot enclosed observation platform at the top. The construction started in February 1963.

When I first visited the construction site, they were digging the foundation. Most of the materials were floated in on barges on the Mississippi River. I made repeated visits, mostly on Sundays, and loved to see the progress being made. Soon I could see two huge concrete footings that were poured way below ground forming the basis for the two legs of the Arch. I would frequent a bar on a riverboat barge moored just below the construction site. From the barge, not only could I observe the progress made on the construction, but I could also enjoy a glass of 3.2 beer and lots of pretzels. At that time, Missouri did not allow the sale of full alcohol on Sundays and that was fine with me.

When I tired of looking at the future Arch, I would watch the boat traffic and daydream of what life was like for Tom Sawyer and Huck Finn a short distance away in Hannibal, Missouri. Since I was always alone, I would strike up conversations with the bartender and other patrons about the Arch and activity on the river. Occasionally, I would meet people who worked on the river and they would tell their tales. I tried to integrate them into my own musings about Tom and Huck.

The Arch construction work was interrupted several times for financial and safety reasons. The large, prefabricated triangles of stainless steel were placed in position by cranes. As the legs started to climb into the sky, they exceeded the height of the cranes. Therefore, they constructed a rail system on the outside of each leg to allow the cranes to move up the completed portion to install the next section. Early observation showed evidence that the two legs would eventually meet. After each new section was secured, an additional section of track was added and the crane moved to a new height. This procedure continued for several iterations until the two legs were about 500 feet high. At that height, a bridge structure was attached to each leg. The bridge added stability for the continued fabrication process. Also incorporated within the bridge were large hydraulic rams which were to be used to spread the legs of the Arch to insert the keystone section. A safety net was also included in the bridge. No fatalities occurred during the entire construction of the Arch.

The morning arrived for the keystone section to be hoisted into position. It was a bright, sunny day and media and dignitaries were all around. The cranes on each leg had cables secured to the keystone section. A flagpole with an American flag was secured to the top of the keystone. The hydraulic rams were activated and the legs were separated and the keystone was about to be inserted. A problem occurred. The bright sun was heating the south leg more than the north leg. The St. Louis fire department was summoned to the site to cool down the south leg. Finally, the keystone was successfully inserted.

It was some time before the Arch was ready for the public to visit. Even after opening, operational issues persisted and people often found themselves stranded in the transport system for hours. Eventually those obstacles were resolved and construction under the Arch continued with a beautiful museum, gift shop, cafeteria, conference rooms, restrooms, and an auditorium where they showed a documentary about the Gateway to the West Arch. I had several wonderful opportunities to go to the observation platform with family and friends. The view is fantastic and breathtaking and the platform sways even in a moderate breeze.

CHAPTER 13
GEMINI

Within my first year at work, I was approached by management to join the Gemini spacecraft team as a Test Engineer on the Environmental Control System (ECS). I moved to Building 3. There was a full-size mockup called the Compatibility Test Unit (CTU) of the Gemini spacecraft complete with wiring, tubing, and wooden boxes shaped like the actual components. We were having great difficulty receiving technical performance and dimensional information about the components from our vendor, Air Research, located in California. My team leader suggested that I go to visit the vendor for three or four days and see what information I could obtain.

I accepted the challenge and told Mrs. Christine I would be gone for a week and flew to Los Angeles. The Air Research engineers met me and gave me a tour of the facility. I acquired preliminary drawings of the components. Every day, I contacted my team leader back in St. Louis and shared the information with him and the team. He told me to mail the drawings and stay a little longer to get more detailed information. The next time I saw him was seven and a half weeks later.

I fell in love with Los Angeles. The climate was pleasant. I enjoyed the beach and the nightlife. I dated several of the secretaries, and really liked one in particular, Gigi. One day she suggested we attend a bullfight in Tijuana, Mexico the following Sunday. Being a farm boy, I was unaccustomed to seeing animals used for sport. However, after a couple of beers and a few bullfights, I was yelling "Ole" along with the crowd. Later, I found out the bulls that were killed were butchered and the meat was given to needy families and that made me less uneasy about the experience.

* * * * * * *

A couple weeks into my stay, I met another McDonnell engineer named Joel who had been sent to LA to work with the vendor on another aspect of the spacecraft. He had a private pilot's license. One day after work we headed out to a small airfield, Hawthorne Aviation, and rented a 2-seater Cessna plane. We flew two touch-and-go patterns for Joel to get familiar with the area and the aircraft. On the third takeoff, we broke the pattern and flew out over LA. It was early evening in the summer and the smog rolled in from over the ocean and blanketed the city. We decided we needed to head back due to the low visibility and Joe asked a profound question, "Where are we?"

I responded with, "Good grief, I have no idea!" He turned back in the direction we believed to be toward the airport and I pulled out the aviation map to try to figure out our location. Between the two of us, we were able to identify a familiar expressway that led back to the airport. While Joel flew along the highway, he radioed the tower to explain our situation. The airport was getting ready to close due to the smog, but they told us they would try to stay open to let us land. If it was not possible, we would have to divert to another airfield. Luckily, we found our way back and immediately after we touched down, the airport closed.

* * * * * * *

I continued gathering information and sending boxes of preliminary drawings back to St. Louis which they were finding very helpful. I began to seriously consider relocating to LA because it was so interesting and entertaining for a young, single fellow. In the end, I returned to St. Louis. I applied to Washington University Graduate School and started a master's degree in mechanical engineering. My first course was Radiation Heat Transfer. McDonnell had a policy that upon successful completion of a course they would reimburse 80% of all expenses: tuition, books, and lab fees. They adjusted employee work schedules to accommodate taking courses. Additionally, upon completing a degree, they reimbursed the remaining 20% of expenses.

* * * * * * *

After about a year and a half, I was put in charge of a team of two engineers and four technicians. Our task was to test ECS components before they were installed in the spacecraft. All the members of the team were older than me and had more seniority at the company. After we set up our facility and established test procedures, we began receiving components from the vendor and performing pre-installation testing. We started with one shift, but soon expanded to two shifts a day. I spent long hours there each day, but it never felt like work; it was fun. My management was impressed with my performance and with every six-month review, I received promotions and raises. I believed my hard work and prayers were paying off.

* * * * * *

Some of my co-workers were jaded and teased me about having "stars in my eyes." They seemed a little jealous of the attention I was receiving from management. They told me eventually I would come around to their way of thinking and only work the mandatory 7:30 am to 4 pm required for my salary. But they didn't know what I knew. They had not endured the grueling work I had in my childhood on the farm. And I had faith that God had special plans for me. I believed that I was utilizing all the resources God gave me and would not be deterred by my coworkers' foolish thinking.

* * * * * *

The ECS components were assembled to produce a system for two astronauts to live and function comfortably while orbiting the earth in a zero gravity, zero pressure, very low temperature environment. I was amazed by the complexity of the design of the components to control the proper pressure, temperature, and oxygen in the capsule and spacesuits as they traveled through the Van Allen radiation belt into orbit. The components also removed elements that could cause discomfort and death such as odor, humidity, and carbon dioxide. The combined knowledge of the men and women that designed and produced the ESC was enormous. And yet, that knowledge was only a very small portion of the knowledge of the entire Gemini space program. That knowledge is a minuscule portion of the known knowledge of mankind, not to mention the knowledge that has yet to be discovered. Every day, mankind discovers new aspects of that infinite supply of knowledge. Infinite knowledge, like infinite energy are attributes of God— the Uncaused Cause. When I pondered these things, I thought about my fourth grade project of constructing the God triangle of the Father, Son, and Holy Spirit and visualized Energy as God the Father and Knowledge as God the Holy Spirit.

* * * * * * *

Now that I was a Team Leader I knew I had to give briefs to different groups of people. However, I always had a fear of public speaking. I took public speaking classes that were offered at McDonell and joined Toastmasters. Another way I learned to conquer my fear was by getting a part in my church's fundraiser play. They needed actors, no experience necessary. I can't remember the name of the play, but the cast included a priest, a nun, and three showgirls. I played the part of a schoolboy. We had three performances: Friday and Saturday evening and a Sunday Matinee. There were many rehearsals, and it was stressful to get up in front of everyone. In the end, it helped me with my fears, and I enjoyed the experience. I never got another opportunity to act, and so far, Hollywood hasn't called.

* * * * * * *

On Friday, November 22, 1963, I was sitting at my desk having lunch when one of the engineers on my team got a telephone call from his wife telling him that the President had been shot in Dallas, Texas. We all hoped and prayed it wasn't too serious and that he would recover. Very little work got done that day. We kept trying to get information. President Kennedy was our hero. We were all working toward his mandate to land a man on the moon and bring him safely back to earth before the end of the decade. Tragically, he died and when we reported to work on Monday the mood was somber as the flag waved at half-mast.

CHAPTER 14
ENTER ZITA

On a Friday in mid-June 1964, after a long, challenging, and tiring week of work, a fellow engineer, John, invited me to attend a dance sponsored by the Cathedral Club, a Catholic organization where he was a member. I told him I was just too tired and didn't want to go. John persisted because there was a girl he wanted to meet and he needed a wing-man. I finally agreed to go if he drove. We arrived at the dance, paid our admission, and entered the hall. We passed a table where six girls were sitting. I told John that one of the girls winked at us and suggested we go back and chat.

We did an about-face swivel on our heels and headed back toward the young ladies at the table. I spotted a sweet looking face that I was immediately attracted to. I grabbed a vacant chair from a neighboring table and sat down next to her. We introduced ourselves and began talking. She was a new member of the club, had just started a new job as a dental assistant, and had just left the convent for the second time. The first time she had entered the convent she left after only a few months because she was so very homesick. After being out for a year, she felt she hadn't given herself sufficient time to determine if being a nun was her vocation. She applied and was accepted to the Daughters of Charity for a second time. After a year, she was convinced religious life was not her vocation.

She was the youngest of seven children, two girls and five boys. She grew up on a small farm in Desoto, Missouri, a town about 40 miles south of St. Louis. When

I met her, she was living with her brother Herb, his wife, and their nine young children in St. Louis. I told her I also grew up on a farm in southwest Michigan and was the oldest of nine children. I told her I graduated two years earlier and was an Engineer at McDonnell Aircraft. Where John was and whether he met up with that girl was very far from my mind. There was an announcement for the last dance, and I asked Zita Marie Witte, "May I have this dance?" While we danced, I asked her for a date the next night and she accepted. I offered her a ride home which she refused. Later, I found out she broke another date to go out with me. She gave me her address. The music stopped and we said good night.

St. Louis, the city, and St. Louis County had a lot of streets named West Park. I spent most of Saturday trying to find the right one. After searching street after street, I still could not find the house number she gave me or the family she described. The last address I went to was in St. Louis very close to Forest Park Zoo. I drove past the house number and saw a lot of little children running around the front yard. I drove the hour and a half back home to North St. Louis County. I cleaned up, dressed, and made the long trip back to pick her up for our date.

I arrived at her brother's house in my brand-new Buick Wildcat. At the door I was greeted by a band of little children who had been told all about this fellow named Tom who was there to pick up their Aunt Zita. They didn't intimidate me, as I had grown up in a house full of little children. I was welcomed in by Zita's sister-in-law Halle and took a seat to wait. I was interrogated by the little army. Thankfully, Zita soon came downstairs from the bedroom she shared with her oldest niece who was a freshman in high school. I wish I could remember where we went that first night. But we must have had a wonderful time because we began seeing a lot of each other after that.

When I took her home, I asked to see her again on Tuesday. She said she would like to, but she was making a Novena to Our Lady of Perpetual Help on Tuesday evenings. I asked if I could join her. She was surprised but happy that I asked to come with her. She told me she was praying to find a good man to marry. Over the next two weeks, we saw each other almost daily. During the Novena, I sang along with the rest of the congregation. She lightly nudged me with her elbow and said, "Ssh, God will understand." I can carry a ton of bricks better than a tune.

The following weekend, my Uncle Jim and Aunt Lillian were coming down from Chicago to visit me. I invited Zita to help me show them St. Louis. We took them around town and ended up on a paddle boat cruise on the Mississippi. My relatives enjoyed her company, she was a delightful hostess. I introduced "Zeets" to them as my date, not my girlfriend. When my aunt and uncle next saw my parents they raved about Tom's wonderful girlfriend. The next weekend I took Zeets to dinner at a local bar and grill for the Friday night special, a lobster tail and baked potato. She was unsure about it as she had never tasted lobster before. I assured her it was very tasty and urged her to give it a try. After one bite, she fell in love with it and it became her entrée of choice accompanied by just one Toasted Almond cocktail.

I was invited to spend a weekend at her parents' farm. They were kind, loving people. Her mother hugged me, and her father shook my hand. I was pleasantly surprised by their greetings as outward signs of affection did not occur in my family. Her father and I bonded over being farmers and he showed me his sheep, rabbits, and gardens. Her mother, unlike my own, was an excellent cook, especially her homemade apple pie. None of her brothers and sisters still lived at home. On the ride back to St. Louis, Zeets told me that her father talked more freely about farm life with me than he did with his own sons.

Zita's childhood home

Zeets was a sweet, charming, young lady who was easy to talk to. She possessed an inner beauty that radiated from her. She had a contagious girlish laugh. Upon hearing her laugh, people would smile or start to laugh themselves, often without knowing the reason for it. I began to think that maybe God had kept this wonderful girl safe for me in the convent so that I could accomplish my goals: an engineering degree and getting established financially and professionally. This was a relationship that needed to be pursued. I was not about to let her get away.

CHAPTER 15
ON THE ROAD

Before Zeets and I met, I planned a three-week road trip to see the Eastern United States with two guys: Jim, a housemate at Mrs. Christine's, and John, the guy who twisted my arm to go to the Cathedral Club dance. When I told Zeets, I got the impression she was looking forward to some time to herself. She wished me well and I told her I would write to her.

At the beginning of July, we hit the road in my Wildcat. We took turns driving and split all the expenses. Our first stop was Louisville, Kentucky, to visit John's mom. We usually traveled at night. One of us would drive while the other two slept. We went to the Mammoth Caves then on to the Natural Bridge and Monticello in Virginia. We spent a few days in both Washington, D.C. and New York City. We saw Connecticut, Massachusetts, Maine, New Hampshire, and Vermont. We even popped over the Canadian border to Quebec and Niagara Falls. We crossed from Windsor to Detroit. At that point, we had covered over 5,000 miles in two weeks. The guys had seen me mail a dozen letters and post cards to Zeets. My thoughts were with her daily. I thought about the past six years and felt that it was God's plan for us to be together. My buddies figured things were getting serious and when I requested their approval to cut the trip short and make a beeline back to St. Louis, they concurred.

* * * * * *

When we arrived back home, my first stop was to see Zeets. I told her that I still had a couple of vacation days left and if she could get a few days off, I would like to take her to meet my family in Michigan. We headed up north putting a few hundred more miles on my Buick. I needed to take the trip to get an indication if she would accept where and how I was raised.

When we arrived at the farm, we were warmly greeted by my parents and all my sisters and brothers. Zeets stayed with my five oldest sisters in their dorm-like bedroom and they really hit it off. They spent hours in friendly girl talk. They wanted to know how we met; did she like me; did she think I liked her. At the time, Dorothy, Jeanne, Pat, and Judy were all seriously dating the men that would become their husbands. I later learned that they had made a pact among themselves that none of them would get married before me.

My Grandma Bartik, and my mother's brother, Uncle Dan, and his wife Aunt Chris came to the farm to spend the weekend (and check out Zeets). It was a joyful, happy weekend. On Sunday we all went to Mass. After the sermon, I gently whispered in her ear, "Will you marry me?" She said yes and I slipped my college class ring on her finger and told her it was only temporary. When we got home from Mass, I told my family we were engaged. My mother cried uncontrollably. My Grandma Bartik hugged Zeets and told her my mother was crying because she was so happy. The next weekend we went to her parents' farm to celebrate the good news with them. I decided that my obligation was to my soon-to-be wife and our family. I stopped sending money to my father. The subject was never brought up by either of us ever again.

When we returned to St. Louis, we went shopping for her engagement ring and our wedding bands. A few weeks later Zeets arranged a reunion at the Daughters of Charity convent in Normandy, Missouri, where she had been preparing for the sisterhood. We met in a reception room. The novices came to meet us in groups. Ladies came and went and talked and I just smiled. Some left and more came and talked and I just smiled. I smiled so much that my face hurt. At future reunions, my presence was not required as Zeets had already shown off her fiancé and ring.

CHAPTER 16
THE WEDDING

I put my advanced education plans on hold and concentrated on my job and Zeets. We were making plans for a June 1965 wedding. Every day after work, I would drive across town to be with her. By the end of the summer, we started thinking about the long winter months ahead and decided to move the wedding date up to November. We knew it had to be before Advent as the Catholic Church did not allow weddings during that time. We zeroed in on the Saturday after Thanksgiving. We hoped the weather would cooperate because my entire family would have to travel from Michigan, Illinois, and Indiana.

We immediately told Zeets' parents because her mother, Martina, was making the gowns for the entire bridal party. Her father thought we were moving ahead too fast, but he soon came around. The matron of honor was Zeets' sister, Katherine. The bridesmaids were my sisters Dorothy and Judy, and Cletis, Zeets' sister-in-law. The junior bridesmaids were my sister Mary and Zeets' niece Stephanie. Our flower girl and ring bearer were Zeets' brother Herb's youngest children, Linda and Herbie. My best man was Zeets' brother Leonard, and the groomsmen were her brother George, brother-in-law Ray, and Judy's fiancé Skip. My little brothers, Robert and Richard, were the Altar servers.

The wedding was set for Saturday, November 28, 1964. As I was the first in my family to marry, all my relatives from up north came down a few days before. Many of them stayed at the homes of the neighbors of

Zeets' parents. My parents and siblings stayed at my future in-laws' house and we all celebrated Thanksgiving together. After work on Friday, I picked up the tuxedos and we decorated the Knights of Columbus Hall for the reception. On Friday night, all the bridesmaids had a sleepover with Zeets and the groomsmen and I stayed at the next-door neighbor's house. A few days before the wedding, I hid my car in a neighbor's barn and drove Zeets' car because her brothers were prone to mischief when it came to decorating a groom's vehicle.

On Saturday morning, I awoke to find that one of the groomsmen hid my shoes. My future mother-in-law interceded on my behalf and got them back in time for the ceremony. The weather was beautiful. It was a late morning Mass at Saint Rose of Lima Catholic Church followed by a luncheon hosted by the church ladies. There were endless photographs. In the evening, we had a reception dinner and dance. After all the gifts were opened and everyone had danced with Zeets, I cut in on my uncle and told her we were dancing out of there. Her brother, George, drove us to my hidden car and we drove to our little three room duplex that I had rented a month before. The next morning, all the out-of-town guests stopped by to see our first little love nest.

Everyone decided to cut their stay short as the weather forecast showed a severe snowstorm moving in. Many guests heading north found themselves following behind paths cut by snowplows. My parents arrived home to the news that Trixie had died on my wedding day. My mother told me that was because she knew her job was complete now that I had a new lady to take care of me. Over the course of the next year and a half, my four oldest sisters all married. Each time, Zeets and I made weekend road trips to attend the weddings.

Tom and Zita's wedding

CHAPTER 17
NEWLYWEDS

Because I had used all my vacation time on the road trip, I had to report back to work on Monday morning so we never had a honeymoon trip. Winter set in and I no longer had the long drive to see Zeets, she was at our home every evening. She continued to work at the dental office. We became involved in our new church, Saint Gregory's and enrolled in a Vatican II study group. Now that I was married to Zeets, I finally broke into the "clannish" St. Louis social scene. We went to monthly potluck dinners and card games with other young couples.

For our first Christmas, I cut down two trees on the Witte's farm. Zeets and I helped her parents decorate their tree. We took ours home and decorated it. We made paper chains and strung popcorn to augment our small supply of store-brought ornaments and lights. Later we went to midnight Mass at St. Gregory's. On Christmas morning, we woke early to spend the day with Zita's parents. Luckily, Saint Gregory's was only a block from our house because the New Year's Eve party was Zeets' first time having more than a drink or two. After midnight, we stumbled home and she complained that the house was galivanting around. She was really hurting. That was the first— and last time— she ever consumed a lot of alcohol.

We continued to frequently spend our weekends with Zeets' elderly parents. I affectionately called them "Popsie" and "Momsie." We helped them with all sorts of chores and odd jobs. Popsie was 75 years old when he walked Zeets down the aisle. We would go on Saturday and after a big dinner we played cards, Pinochle with a double deck. What Popsie loved more than playing cards was watching the news, Lawrence Welk, and wrestling on TV. When he watched wrestling, we all watched his reactions. He sat in a hard-backed dining room chair right next to the TV screen. He would get so excited that sometimes chairs would get tipped over and drinks were spilled. Often we feared he would have a heart attack. We would stay overnight and take them to Mass on Sunday morning. They were very affectionate with one another and me. I was not used to all the hugging as my family was not demonstrative with their affection. I told Zeets all the time that she taught me how to hug and I called her Pumpkin. Popsie was the Dad I never had.

* * * * * *

One night at our home, we started talking about our childhood experiences. Zeets had a happy childhood as the baby of the family with loving parents and siblings. When I tried telling her about things that happened to me, I choked up and couldn't speak. She came to me and wrapped her arms around me and told me it was okay to cry. I wept and wept. It was the first time in my life I cried. I am sure I cried as an infant, but I have no memory of it. I remember being very sad at my Gramps' funeral, but even then I didn't cry. I learned early on not to cry when I was injured or beaten and held it in my entire life. Suddenly, the floodgates were opened.

* * * * * *

One of the guys in our church study group, Don, also taught the freshman and sophomore high school boys Sunday school. He convinced me to be his assistant. A couple of weeks into it, he had to go out of town and asked me to take over the class. I figured it couldn't be that hard because there was a prepared syllabus and lesson plans. What the course material didn't cover was how to control a bunch of teenaged boys. The experience convinced me I was never going to try to teach young men anything ever again.

* * * * * *

One freezing cold night in January 1965, after my shift on the rescue team, I arrived home about 3 am. Zeets was asleep, so I quietly began to undress when I heard a tremendous sound. My first thought was that an overworked gas furnace had exploded. The blast was so great it shook our picture of *The Last Supper* off the kitchen wall. I checked to be sure it wasn't our furnace then I ran outside half-dressed to find out what happened. Two houses down on the corner, a car was leaning against the street light post with the rear bumper in the air. In the intersection were two clumps of what appeared to be debris. As I walked closer, I realized one of the clumps was a man. He was bleeding profusely from a deep cut in his neck.

I ran back home and Zeets was now awake. I asked her for a blanket to cover the man and told her to call an ambulance (the 911 system was not yet in place). I went back and covered the man. By that time, several residents were gathered. One suggested we move the man indoors because of the cold. I told them if we tried to move him we could make his injuries worse. Someone mentioned that they knew the injured man and he was a Catholic. I ran to the St. Gregory rectory and woke the housekeeper and a priest and told them what had happened. The priest came to give the man his Last Rites.

When I returned to the accident site, the crowd was much larger and the police were there. There was nothing more I could do. I returned home and Zeets told me an ambulance was on the way. I figured the man had been traveling too fast, lost control, and hit a fire hydrant which ripped off the rear axle. Later, I called the hospital to try and get information and was informed that he was in critical condition, but they could not give me any more details. All Zeets and I could do was pray for him.

* * * * * * *

At work, I volunteered to be on the four-man rescue team for the Gemini program. The spacecraft with two astronauts in full space suits was placed in a 30-foot vacuum chamber. The pressure in the chamber simulated the orbital pressure of space. The rescue team, equipped with oxygen masks, was in an adjoining chamber with simulated altitude pressure of 27,000 feet. If a medical emergency occurred in the astronauts' chamber, it was rapidly brought down to sea level pressure. While that was occurring, the pressure in the rescue team chamber was being equalized to match the astronauts' chamber. The rescue team would enter the main chamber, open the spacecraft hatch, and with the aid of a hoisting system, remove the astronauts, put them on stretchers, and carry them out. Two rescue team members were assigned to each astronaut. I worked with Gus Grissom, Wally Schirra, Ed White, Jim Lovell, John Young, Gordon Cooper, Frank Bormn, Thomas Stafford, Pete Conrad, Gene Cernan, James McDivitt, Richard Gordon, Jr., Buzz Aldrin, and Neil Armstrong. At every test, there was a team of doctors and nurses outside the chambers constantly monitoring the astronauts' vital signs. Safety was the number one priority. We never had a single mishap. In fact, the only accident during the Gemini program was the horrible T-38 crash on February 28, 1966.

* * * * * *

It was mid-morning and I was in building 103 working with the medical doctor preparing for our next test when we heard a loud crash. We ran outside and saw a large amount of billowing smoke. We ran up the hill toward building 101. We saw an aircraft twisted in a pile of construction steel that was being used to build the new buildings, 104 and 105. The fire and rescue team from Lambert Field airport arrived. The scene was gruesome. One pilot had been thrown from the cockpit still strapped in his ejection seat. I saw a helmet lying on the ground. The pilot strapped in the seat was Elliot See. Charles Bassett had been decapitated on impact. The doctor said there was nothing we could do and we should leave.

Two aircraft had departed Ellington Air Force Base in Texas headed for Lambert Field to conduct training in the Gemini docking simulator. In the lead aircraft, Elliot See was at the controls and Charles Bassett was in the rear seat. The plane, in the wing position, was piloted by Tom

Stafford with Gene Cernan in the rear. The weather was poor with rain, snow, and fog and the pilots were required to make an instrument approach. Initially, both pilots missed the outer maker and overshot the runway. See then elected to make a visual circling approach; however, Stafford opted to follow standard procedure for a second missed approach. See's aircraft was off the glidepath that ran north of building 103. His approach was too low, and the landing gear clipped the edge of building 101, damaging the building and causing minor injuries to workers inside. The aircraft did a cartwheel into a pile of construction steel. See and Bassett died 500 feet from the spacecraft they were training to fly. It was in the final stages of assembly in building 101. The subsequent investigation led by Alan Shepard concluded that the crash was caused by pilot error.

CHAPTER 18
CHANGE OF CAREER FOCUS

While studying engineering at Marquette, I focused on a career in mechanical technology research with an emphasis in nuclear engineering research. Additionally, I gave serious consideration to a career path of hands-on testing in non-nuclear fields. The job applications I submitted during my senior year were with these goals in mind. I wanted to further my education and obtain a post-graduate degree in a technical discipline to further enhance my prospects in the research arena, but my first desire was gaining experience as an engineer.

Managing a team of technical professionals in performing hands-on hardware testing gave me great pleasure and satisfaction. I realized I had control of a scope of activity greater than what I could accomplish alone. I enjoyed the "macro" more than the "micro," while still managing the micro. I was successful at solving managerial issues including personnel challenges and implementing operational changes that improved performance and productivity and saved the company money.

My management liked my performance and the changes I initiated. I didn't hesitate to accept functions that made their jobs easier and gave me the opportunity to learn what was required at the next level. Accordingly, I was promoted and awarded salary increases. My superiors told me that my name was routinely mentioned at staff meetings when they were considering filling management positions.

I was doing exactly what I wanted, and I was comfortable with the direction my career was headed. Furthering my education at night in a master's in business administration (MBA) program specializing in quantitative analysis would give me the additional knowledge and skills to continue to excel. Also, it would signal to management my desire for growth and promotion. I was motivated toward my next goal: the St. Louis University MBA program.

CHAPTER 19
STARTING OUR FAMILY

Zeets and I wanted to start our family immediately. I was financially stable and we both loved children. We loved their innocence and purity. We couldn't wait to experience the joy and unconditional love we knew they would bring. We also believed that children help adults grow emotionally. We were ready to undertake the tremendous responsibility of raising them to become the future.

Zeets' period was frequently late, many times as much as a month, but she wasn't getting pregnant. She went to see her OB/GYN and he conducted many tests: at first on me and then on her. None of the tests disclosed any problem. The doctor suggested fertility drugs, but because of the potential side effects, including diabetes, I left the decision up to Zeets. She decided to take the drugs despite the risks. Years later, we reflected on her myriad of health issues, including her diabetes, and wondered if they were caused by the drugs. After about two and a half years, the doctor encouraged us to consider adopting. Zeets and I prayed. We went to Catholic Charities and filled out applications and got letters of recommendation from our parents and our Pastor. We were still trying and over and over we would get our hopes up only to have them dashed again.

Catholic Charities had many requirements. There were a lot of in-depth interviews of us and our parents. They wanted to know as much as possible about our family histories and educational backgrounds to match us as closely as possible with an infant's parents. We didn't care if we got a boy or a girl. We told them we wanted whatever God sends us. And then the waiting began. We kept trying to conceive. There were many doctor visits and Zeets was still taking medication. We waited and waited. A social worker came to visit our three-room duplex and we assured her that as soon as a baby was on the way, we planned to buy a larger house. Zeets continued to work as a dental assistant and I continued on a glide path of promotions and salary increases.

While we were waiting, we were deciding on names. If we were blessed with a son, I wanted to give him the greatest gift I could think of— my name. He would be Thomas Joseph Pojeta, Jr. If we were blessed with a daughter, we agreed to name her after our mothers, Martina Rose and call her Tina. Zeets wanted to start amassing baby things, but since we had no idea on gender, I suggested not getting too many clothing items yet. However, we started hunting for a house. As luck would have it, when Zeets' sister Kate and her husband Ray moved from Kansas City to St Louis, they purchased a small two-bedroom home for their family. Kate and Ray had four children. Very soon they realized the house was too small and they were looking for a larger home. We thought it would make an ideal starter home for us and brought it.

* * * * * * *

As soon as we moved in, Zeets started turning the second bedroom into a nursery. My project was to renovate the unfinished basement including a laundry room, a sewing room for Zeets, a small workshop for me, a full bathroom, and a large Rec Room with a bar. I had to work steadily at it since Zeets wanted to have the family Thanksgiving dinner there. Once I got the studs for the walls up and the electricity wired, Zeets' parents came to stay for several days and Popsie helped put in the paneling. We succeeded in completing the project in time for the holidays.

* * * * * *

Meanwhile, at work I was asked if I would be interested in managing the calibration lab. I was flattered that they had such confidence in me. The position entailed a large increase in personnel and equipment. The lab was tasked with determining the accuracy of all instrumentation used to measure the testing performance of the spacecraft and aircraft systems. I accepted and took on the supervision of 47 personnel: two engineers, five senior-lead technicians, and 40 technicians on three shifts. Just like my previous assignment, I really enjoyed the management and leadership responsibilities. I decided on a new career goal, to move away from technical aspects to management of technical personnel. I requested approval and funding support to pursue a master's degree in business administration (MBA).

* * * * * *

I was accepted at St. Louis University College of Business Administration and enrolled in classes two nights a week. Shortly thereafter, we received the news we had been praying for. We were getting a baby girl. She had been born on August 22, 1968. At Catholic Charities, there was a transition period after an infant's birth where he or she was placed with a foster family for a brief time. Zeets began shopping for little pink things for the nursery and the baby. Martina Rose was baptized at the St. Louis National Cathedral. Later we had a Baptismal celebration and Kate and Ray were her Godparents.

The day came to bring her home. Her foster mother brought Tina into the "Baby Room" where all adoptive parents met their babies for the first time. We could hear her before we ever saw her. When we entered the room, she was laying in the little wooden bassinet that every baby being adopted was placed in. She was the most beautiful baby I had ever seen: a blue-eyed, blonde angel. Zeets immediately picked her up and held her. I wanted to hold her, too, but was secretly afraid I might break her, plus Zeets showed no sign of letting her go anytime soon. When I finally held her, it was the most wonderful feeling I had ever experienced.

Once we left the adoption agency, I pointed out everything we passed and told Tina what everything was called. I said, "This is our car," and "That is a bicycle." There were no seat belts or car seats at that time, so Zeets held her in her arms all the way home where I informed Tina, "This is your home." When we pulled into the driveway, the older childless couple across the street, who asked us to call them Papa Bill and Mamma Bill were there to greet us. The minute they laid eyes on Tina, they dubbed her with the nickname "Baby Dumpling." My usually shy and reserved wife was talking non-stop.

The following weekend, we had a baby shower for Tina. Even though Tina had her own room filled with baby furniture, Zeets kept her in a little bassinet beside her all the time. When we went to sleep at night, little Tina was right next to our bed. We waited a long time for that little lady and we were not about to let anything happen to her. My special time with Tina was her late-night bottle. I would hum a lullaby to her as she drank because I feared my singing would disturb her. On the nights I had class, it was the first thing I did when I returned home. Zeets had heard that music was soothing to infants so we purchased a stereo and classical music albums to comfort Tina.

However, we still had a long road ahead of us. There was a probationary period of one year before the adoption could be finalized. A social worker visited us at least once a month, sometimes scheduled and sometimes impromptu, to check on our home and the health and welfare of little Tina. Zeets stopped working as soon as we got Tina and was now a full-time stay-at-home mother and homemaker.

Once Tina could sit up in my lap, I would read books to her and we would play with educational toys and games. She liked to sit on my lap when I did my homework. In my top drawer, I had little pencil erasers in the shapes of animals. She loved to line them up and rearrange them. This would often keep her amused the entire time it took to complete my assignment.

When Tina was one year old we went to court for the adoption hearing. The Judge asked me what nationality Pojeta was and when I told him, he started to speak

Czech. I had to admit to him that I knew almost no Czech. The social worker testified about her interactions with us over the past year. Everything went smoothly and it was official. We were given a birth certificate for Martina Rose Pojeta. We were her father and mother.

Martina Rose at one year old

When Tina was just over a year old, she and Zeets enrolled in the YMCA Water Babies course. Tina learned to walk and swim at the same time. Zeets and I discussed applying for another child to adopt even as she continued with fertility treatments. We quickly determined whether she got pregnant or we adopted again, or both, we would soon outgrow our tiny two-bedroom home. We started to look at model homes in new suburban housing developments.

We found ourselves repeatedly going back to a neighborhood called Paddock Forest in North St. Louis County. We fell in love with one model: a four-bedroom Colonial Ranch. One of the bedrooms was decorated with toys for young children. Every time we visited the model, Tina made a beeline for the "toy room." The developer was opening a new section of construction and the lot we liked backed to a common area with a small lake. We decided to build the model house on that lot. Zeets was apprehensive. She didn't believe we could afford it, but I reassured her that it was within our budget.

CHAPTER 20
MAJOR CHANGES

Just before we put down our deposit, we applied for a second adoption. We had the same social worker that helped us adopt Tina. The only request we had was that we really would like a baby boy. When we adopted the first time, we decided we would name a son Thomas Joseph Pojeta, Jr. Zeets was concerned that if she got pregnant and we had a second boy the Junior moniker would be taken. I told her we would cross that bridge if, or when, we came to it.

* * * * * *

The timing of the new house construction and adoption was good. The social worker told us that based on the birth rates at the time and our request for a boy, it would be at least a year for a baby to become available for adoption. We were okay with that because it would give us time for our new house to be built, to sell our current house, and move. However, all our best laid plans would not happen on schedule. We signed the contract for the new house and were informed it would take six to nine months after the loan approval to complete.

We put our house up for sale "By Owner." We made signs, advertised in the paper, and had an open house. Although there was a lot of interest and many people showed up, I soon found out it wasn't going to be easy to sell it myself. A few weeks later, a gentleman named Rick, who had come to the open house, became a realtor and was just starting his own business. He asked if he could list our house. He seemed ethical and eager. We signed a contract with him with the provision that we could rent it back until our new house was completed.

The next day after I came home from work, Zeets went shopping and I was taking care of Tina. Rick called and asked if he could bring a couple by to see the house. I told him Zeets was out, Tina had toys everywhere, and the sink was full of dirty dishes. Rick assured me it was fine and that he would be over in a half hour. I scrambled to tidy up as much as I could before they arrived exactly 30 minutes later. They went through the entire first floor then the downstairs, where they stayed a very long time. It was dark and they didn't even look around outside before they left.

When Zeets came home, I told her what had happened. Just after we put Tina to bed, Rick called to tell us he had an offer. The couple accepted all our terms but wanted to close and take possession in June. It was April and the new house construction hadn't even started. I called Paddock Forest and was assured that they could have the house built 90 days after the foundation was laid. The new owners were adamant that they needed an early June move in date so that the wife could have the house entirely settled before she started teaching in the fall. We decided to take the risk and signed the contract.

The ink on the contract had not yet dried when we were informed that our new house construction would be delayed because of a concrete workers' strike. We tried to stay positive, and hope that the strike would end quickly and not interfere with our plans. However, that was not the case. It dragged on for weeks. To boost our morale, we stopped at the model dream house every chance we could and let Tina play in the toy room.

We told the buyer's agent of our predicament and asked to rent our house until the new one was built, but they refused and wanted to stick to the terms of the contract. We approached the sales team at Paddock Forest for help. The builder owned an apartment complex just blocks from our new house and offered us a furnished unit that was available on a month-to-month lease.

When we moved, we packed our clothes and stored almost everything else. I brought a very old used Ford F-150 truck to do the job. In the meantime, we kept in constant communication with the social worker at Catholic Charities about our next adoption. The apartment turned out to be a great experience. Zeets and Tina started meeting our neighbors. We joined the Bath and Tennis Club and went to the pool in the evenings after work. Tina was a YMCA Water Baby and though she wasn't even two years old, she was a proficient swimmer. One day she jumped in the deep end of the pool and a gentleman tanning poolside berated Zeets for being a poor mother for risking her baby drowning. Zeets assured him, if need be, her toddler could probably rescue him! We also joined our new parish, Transfiguration, and started going to Mass there and meeting our fellow parishioners.

A few months later the strike was settled and they broke ground on the construction. Just about every day I would stop by the site and monitor the progress. On

Fridays after work, I would bring a cooler of beer to the crew. They appreciated the gesture and it went a long way to ensure everything went smoothly. One example was they relocated the entrance to the family room because I thought it would be better than the original plans. Before the drywall went up, they let me run speaker wires in the walls.

* * * * * *

That summer, Tina attended her first graduation ceremony. I had completed all the requirements for my MBA and was content to have my diploma mailed to me. However, Zeets would not entertain any discussion on the issue and insisted I walk at my graduation ceremony for the entire family to witness. She also wanted to host a party at our apartment with our friends and relatives to celebrate my achievement. I had no problem acquiescing to her request. For three years, I took classes, studied on nights and weekends, made countless trips to the library and computer lab while she sacrificed doing things she would have enjoyed supporting my effort. She made it a lovely occasion and I cherish the memory.

Tom at his MBA graduation

I figured that I had enough schooling for a while and we turned our attention to Zeets' education. She had always wanted to become a nurse. Additionally, it would provide her a security blanket if I died or lost my job. She found a nighttime Certificate of Nursing Program at Maryville College in Town and Country, Missouri. She applied and was accepted. She attended classes two nights a week while I took care of Tina.

Finally, the day arrived and our house was ready for occupancy. We moved in and set up our bedrooms and hung sheets as temporary window treatments. We had no furniture for the formal living room or dining room, those would have to wait until we completed the nursery for our future baby boy. Once we were settled in, our social worker made her required visits to inspect our living quarters.

* * * * * *

On August 12, 1970, we were informed that Tommy, Jr. was born. Just as had happened with Tina, he was initially placed with a foster family. Tina was thrilled that the playmate, the baby brother she had been promised, was finally here. As we waited in the reception room, we heard a baby wailing and wondered if that was him. It was. He had the strongest set of lungs. We were led to the same room where we first saw Tina and Tommy laying in the same little crib she had used. Tina walked over and peered in. She seemed disappointed and commented that he was too little to play with. Just as it had been with Tina, Tommy had all his worldly possessions with him. His blanket, bottles, and stuffed animals. We could just feel the love and care that the foster mothers had given to our babies.

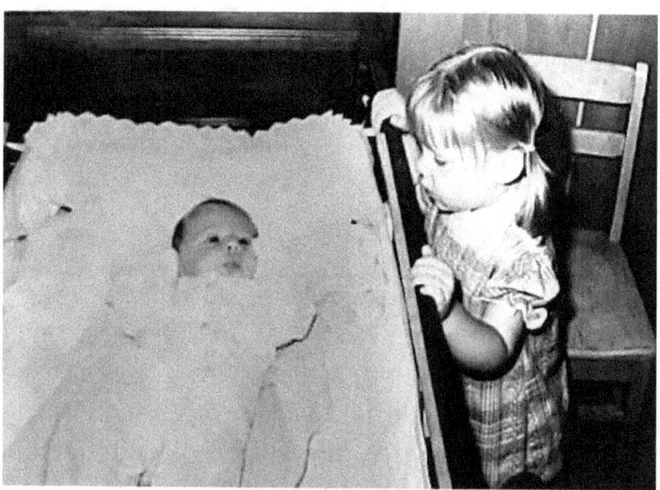

Tina meets Tommy

Tommy had impeccable timing. Without fail, anytime Zeets would leave the house for any errand, he would fill his diaper. He was such a skinny baby, it was hard to get a diaper to stay put. I became an expert at changing and cleaning him. Just like Tina before him, Tommy had been baptized at the St. Louis National Cathedral. Within a few weeks, we had a baptismal ceremony for him at Transfiguration. My sister Mary and brother Robert were his Godparents. Both sets of grandparents and many other relatives came and we had our first big celebration in our new home.

And just like I did with Tina, every night I fed Tommy his bedtime bottle. That was our special time. The difference was that Tommy would throw up every time he was burped. I had to use the biggest towel we had to protect myself. Tina took some issue with having her Dada's attention divided between her and another child. As soon as Tommy started to pull himself up to walk alongside the coffee table, he developed an interesting habit. If Tina was anywhere near him, he immediately sat down. This was his defense mechanism because every time Tina saw him stand up, she would push him down. Zeets and I were concerned that he would never learn how to walk.

* * * * * * *

Zeets and I were committed to our parental responsibilities. We filled the house with educational toys and we constantly read books to the children. Soft, uplifting music was always on the stereo in the background. Early on we noticed something wrong with Tommy's right eye. The pediatrician advised us to monitor the situation to see if it improved or worsened. Eventually, he was diagnosed with Amblyopia, a condition where the nerve pathways between the brain and the eye are not properly stimulated, and the brain favors one eye over the other.

We took him to an eye specialist who said we first needed to determine if he could see out of his right eye. After it was determined he could, we needed to build up the muscles in his injured eye. Therefore, he had to wear an eyepatch on his left eye to force him to use the weak right eye. Tommy did not care for this arrangement and he would frequently peek out from under his eyepatch to see what he was missing. After a while, the eye surgeon told us it was time to operate on his eye muscles.

We prayed and cried all through the surgery. I would have given anything to trade places with him. When he was in recovery, he could not stop trying to scratch at his bandaged eye. It was heart-wrenching to see him suffer. After the surgery, he had to keep a patch on his good eye again. However, by the time he started school, he had virtually lost his vision in his right eye. His vision was 20/300 and uncorrectable.

* * * * * *

As a toddler, Tommy started to develop severe, debilitating headaches. His pediatrician referred us to several specialists, but none of them were able to determine the cause. Finally, a neurologist suggested that we not allow Tommy to eat chocolate. The unhappy young boy was weaned off his favorite food and in a short time, his headaches disappeared. Tommy was a believer but occasionally would test the theory by sneaking some. Eventually, he accepted that not eating chocolate would be a lifelong commitment. Over 50 years later, if he even has a taste of chocolate, he pays the price with a headache.

* * * * * *

I drove the beat-up Ford F-150 truck to work so that Zeets would have the family car for her and the kids. Zeets emphatically stipulated that every afternoon when I was leaving the office I had to call home so that she could open the garage door. I was ordered to drive my junk of a truck in and immediately close the garage door so that the neighbors wouldn't see it! I also used the truck for landscaping around the house and hauling supplies to build a patio, a pond with a waterfall, and a built-in barbecue pit.

We loved that outdoor space and hosted many BBQs and wine and cheese parties with the neighbors. Later when Tina and Tommy got a little older, we added an above-ground pool. It attracted all the kids' friends and Zeets found herself acting as babysitter and lifeguard for the neighborhood. To cut down on the numbers, she required each child to bring a note from a parent stating it was okay for them to swim. That was hardly a deterrent, every child continued to come note in hand. Zeets' next attempt at crowd control was to require that each little swimmer come accompanied by a parent and the number of children drastically diminished.

After several years, the pool deteriorated and Zeets wanted to replace it with an in-ground pool. I was opposed. We discussed what would be required to maintain it, as well as the liability and insurance issues. I suggested we take the money and purchase a family membership to the Bath & Tennis Club we used when we lived in the apartment. It was within walking distance from the house, the children could join the swim team, and we could socialize with our friends and neighbors after work and on the weekends. She remained unconvinced that it would be as good as a backyard pool, but with a little more persuasion, she agreed to try it. It worked out great and we ended up loving it. Zeets would pack a little picnic and some cocktails for our worry- free relaxation time. Tina and Tommy did join the swim team and became excellent swimmers. After each swim meet, the children loved to go to the local McDonalds for victory treats.

* * * * * *

In the late 1960s, the Douglas Aircraft Corporation was experiencing financial trouble. McDonnell had always wanted to get into commercial aircraft manufacturing. When the merger took place, the McDonnell employees were advised that austerity would kick in. Additionally, many McDonnell employees were going to be transferred to the Douglas facility in Southern California. My supervisor told me if I were interested, I could transfer. I gave it serious consideration. Our life was firmly established in St. Louis, Zeets' entire extended family was there, and I was working on my MBA at St. Louis University. However, the offer gave me insight into my company's plans to develop me for greater managerial positions.

* * * * * * *

At that time, I was also working on providing wind tunnel data on a next generation high performance fighter aircraft for the Air Force, the F-15. Everyone at McDonnell felt we could afford to absorb the financial challenge of acquiring Douglas because of the tremendous F-4 sales and the anticipated sales of the F-15. We had been awarded the contract in 1969.

* * * * * * *

I oversaw the electro-mechanical section of the calibration laboratory. I supervised five lead technicians, one engineer, and over 40 technicians who were tasked with calibrating all the electro-mechanical instrumentation company wide. In 1970 and 1971, the U.S. began withdrawing from Viet Nam and the defense industry felt the impact. The F-15 contract was reduced. I was forced to lay off employees. Every other week I had to give one of my subordinates a "pink slip." As my colleagues were laid off, I was given many of their responsibilities.

I kept telling Zeets that one day soon they would be giving me a pink slip. I polished up my resumé and began looking for other opportunities. Zeets graduated and was employed as a Registered Nurse at St. John's Hospital awaiting the successful outcome of her exam with the state licensing board. Finally, the day arrived on a Friday in June 1974. They gave me two weeks' notice (two weeks more than all the employees I had to let go). On Monday at work, the word was out that Pojeta got his pink slip. One of my colleagues mentioned that Army

Aviation had direct hire authority and they were looking for engineers being laid off by McDonnell Douglas. That day, I gave Army Aviation Human Resources a call and was invited for an interview on Wednesday.

* * * * * * *

I was interviewed by three Branch Chiefs and offered an engineering position in the Aviation Maintenance Branch in St. Louis. They offered me the highest salary they had for direct hires; a GS-11 Step 1. I had no issue with the grade of GS-11 but requested a higher step to be closer to the salary I was currently making. They said they would go back to the Civil Service Commission and request a higher step. They told me to check back with them at the end of the week because their hiring authority expired that Friday. On Thursday, Zeets left for Jefferson City to sit for her RN Board exam.

Ever since the company had started layoffs, I began looking for other opportunities. Over a period of two years, I sent out over 40 resumés. I had been communicating with two other companies, Boise Cascade in St. Louis and Motorola in Schaumburg, Illinois. Both positions were at a higher salary than I was currently making. I was shown offices described as "Bigelow on the floor and your name on the door."

On Friday afternoon, I called Army Aviation HR and was informed that they could not get an exception to the current hiring authority even though my SF-171 (Application) was evaluated and graded out for a GS14/15 engineering position. I respectfully declined the offer. I still had a week at McDonnell Douglas and I thought one of the other companies would make an offer. The only other option was unemployment benefits, which paid $58.00 a week. Zeets returned home Friday night. After the children were tucked in their beds, we sat down to talk. I told her everything that transpired and she had a sweet way of bringing me back to reality.

She said, "You are going to be hell to live with!" She predicted I would be sitting by the phone waiting for it to ring and wearing out a path to the mailbox hoping for news of a job offer. She pointed out that even though the GS-11/1 salary was a lot less than I was currently making, it was a lot more than $58.00 a week. Additionally, she reminded me that I would not be obligated to stay in the government job for any specific amount of time. I could leave if, or when, a better offer came along.

I had a difficult time trying to get any sleep that night. I knew the hiring authority had already expired. When I woke up on Saturday morning, it was a beautiful sunny day. After a cup of coffee and replaying my conversation with Zeets over and over in my mind, I went to the closet and pulled out the St. Louis telephone directory. I hoped the Human Resources Specialist's home phone number was listed, and thankfully, it was.

At 10 am I called Bernadette. When she answered, I identified myself and said, "Can I invoke a woman's prerogative to change my mind?" Bernadette said, "Absolutely." On Monday, she would date my paperwork accepting the position for Friday and asked me when I would like to report to work. I told her I had a week left at my old job and would like to report the following Monday.

She told me that was too soon to get anything to me in writing, but to report that day at 9 am to complete all the onboarding documentation.

That phone call began my 38-year career with the Department of Defense. I continued to explore those two other prospects, but no job offers ever materialized. Nine months later, McDonnell Douglas called me back to work. At that time, my prospects for promotions with the government were looking very good. I was still hurt from being laid off from the company to which I had been so loyal. I figured if they did it once, what would prevent them from doing it again. I thanked them and respectfully declined their offer.

1975-1981

THE END OF AN ERA

CHAPTER 21
ARMY AVIATION

Immediately after assuming my new position as a Maintenance Engineer on the UH-1 Huey and AH-1 Cobra helicopters, I was sent to Corpus Christi, Texas, to the Army Depot for two weeks to learn how to repair and maintain the two aircraft. About six months later, on a Monday morning, my Branch Chief Ron told me there was a mishap on a UH-1 the week before. Therefore, Bell Helicopter was giving a presentation on a proposed modification to the rotor warning systems. My assignment was to be the government's Project Engineer.

I asked about the mishap and was told there was a malfunction in the RPM of the main rotor warning system. He had no information other than a presentation that was scheduled to begin in 30 minutes. I went into our file system and grabbed the blueprints of the rotor warning system. We went into our huge conference room where there were over 50 people. Ron had a seat at the table, and I sat behind him along the wall. The Bell Helicopter team gave their presentation for a totally new warning system that included a complete re-qualification of the UH-1 and AH-1 aircraft.

The presentation addressed the failure of one signal of a redundant warning system. Before the mishap, the RPM warning light came on and audible alarms sounded. The pilot did exactly what he was trained to do: he reduced pitch of the main rotor blade to increase RPM speed as he descended. A few hundred feet above the ground, he increased pitch to reduce the rotor RPM which greatly increased his descent. However, he had settled the helicopter in rough terrain, and as it rocked from side to side, a brigadier general was ejected out of the back seat. The general, who wasn't wearing a seatbelt, suffered a broken arm.

Analysis of the situation disclosed that there was no main rotor failure at all. A wire to the sensor came loose and triggered the alarms. The proposal was to take the signals from the two sensors, both of which were attached to the same mechanical powertrain, and integrate them. The estimated cost was millions of dollars. The modifications would be done by the prime contractor and paid for with taxpayer dollars.

* * * * * * *

Being new, I was not aware of the protocol and innocently raised my hand. Over 100 eyeballs swiveled in my direction. I said, "I have the blueprint of that system on my lap and looking at the functionality of that system, it appears to me that what's really needed is to take the signal from the existing two sensors and incorporate it into a NAND gate whereby both signals would have to be missing to activate the alarms." The Bell Helicopter team stopped their presentation. They said they would evaluate my suggestion and get back to the government. The meeting was concluded.

Ron and I went back to my desk and he asked if I was sure about what I said. I rolled out the blueprints and showed him. Later that day, the Director of Army Aviation Product Assurance and Reliability, told Ron that his facility and his staff at Granite City, Illinois, were available to verify and implement my suggestion on two UH-1 helicopters. The next morning, I reported to my new duty station at Granite City and briefed the technical staff on the plan. I was amazed by their enthusiasm. They retrieved the RPM warning boxes and began analyzing the circuits. That evening after work, one of the engineers stopped at Radio Shack and for less than $5.00 procured the electrical components needed to complete the task.

The next day the components were mounted on a circuit board and placed in the RPM warning box which was then installed in one of the helicopters. The aircraft maintenance chief started the helicopter. A false "No Signal" was duplicated at each of the sensors by disconnecting the wires to the sensors. When one of the sensors was disconnected, no audible or visual alarm was triggered. However, when both sensors were disconnected, the audio and visual alarms were activated. With that information, my Branch Chief briefed his superiors and received authorization to proceed with the modification on the entire fleet of UH-1 and AH-1 helicopters of over 10,000 aircraft.

Next, I worked on designing the kit that would be used for the modification. Several kits were produced and put through environmental testing at a private contractor in New Jersey. After successful testing, I met with the staff tasked to write the procedures for the field installation of the kits. Funds were appropriated and authorized to proceed with bid proposals for fabrication of over 10,000 kits. The New York Penal System, the lowest bidder, was awarded the contract. Every week, I had to brief the officer in charge of the operational status of the UH-

1/AH-I fleet. We got to know each other and had many enjoyable chats. His name was Colonel John W. Pershing, III, the grandson of the famed WWI general "Black Jack" Pershing. Many years later, I did the arithmetic and determined my fix saved the taxpayers enough money to pay my salary for the entire 38 years I worked for the government.

My team leader put me in for a Quality Step Increase as a bonus for my work. Shortly after that, I was promoted to GS-12 and given a new job evaluating the reliability of aircraft components. Around that time, I finished my master's degree in electrical engineering from University of Missouri. One of my first tasks was to work on a solution to eliminate the vibration caused when replacing one of the two rotor blades during the overhaul of the helicopters. I saw this challenge as a potential research topic for a PhD dissertation.

CHAPTER 22
VISITING THE FARM

Every year, we had a goal to visit my parents a couple times. We weren't always able to do so, but we always visited at least once each summer. My mother looked forward to it for two reasons. First, she adored her grandchildren, and they absolutely loved her. Second, Zeets would bring everything needed and cook for the entire visit, except for my mom's specialty, homemade rye bread. My mom always wanted to know what time we were planning to arrive so that she could be pulling the bread out of the oven as we were pulling into the driveway. As soon as we opened the car doors, we were hit with that magnificent aroma.

Tina and Tommy would follow my mother like a shadow when she fed the chickens and gathered the eggs. The children demanded a tractor ride everyday it didn't rain. It seemed there was always a litter of kittens when we visited. Tina was overjoyed to cuddle and play with them. One summer there was a special treat, a brown and white calf was born during our visit. Tina and Tommy were thrilled with how the mama cow took such care of her baby. There was much discussion on what we should name the baby. I can't remember if it was a male or female, but every name you can imagine was considered. Finally, my mother decreed that Tina would have the honor of naming the baby cow. After much deliberation, the calf was christened "Peaches."

Tina and Tommy on the farm

After we left that summer, Tina would call my mom and ask about Peaches and whenever my mom wrote us a letter she would include a paragraph to Tina on the latest adventures of Peaches. The following summer when we arrived at the farm, Tina and Tommy threw open the car doors and bolted to the barn. Much to Tina's disappointment, Peaches was no longer an adorable calf but rather an almost full-grown cow.

* * * * * * *

One day, my mother, Zeets, my sister Mary, and Tina planned to visit my sister Dorothy and her husband Ed at their new home. I wasn't feeling well and had been taking antibiotics for a few days. I decided to stay at the farm and Tommy wanted to stay with me. My brother Bob still lived at home, and he was in the field baling hay. Bob brought a load of hay up by the barn then hopped in his truck to go visit his girlfriend who lived nearby.

My father was furious. The sky was threatening rain and he wanted the hay in the barn so it wouldn't get wet. My father could not comprehend why a teenaged boy would leave a chore unfinished to go visit a girl. Even though I was not feeling well, I suggested I could unload the bales of hay onto the conveyor belt outside the barn if my father would go into the barn and stack them as they came in. My father went into the barn and I turned on the conveyor. The clutch malfunctioned and the belt wasn't moving. I tried to move the clutch lever and my hand slipped into the belt. Half of my pinkie finger on my left hand was traumatically amputated and my ring finger was injured.

I yelled to my father who came down and saw what happened. We searched for the missing part of my finger but couldn't find it. I held my injured fingers tightly with my right hand to stem the bleeding. Tommy wanted to see so I opened my hand and showed him. My father ran to the house to get the truck keys and drove us to the emergency room. The doctor cleaned my wounds and sewed my pinkie finger closed and bandaged my hand. I wasn't angry; it could have been worse. Well, I figured I could still give a "high five" with my right hand and a "high four and a half" with my left. When the bandages came off and my hand healed, I realized that my typing ability was severely diminished. Shortly after we returned from the ER, my mother, Zeets, Mary, and Tina arrived home from their trip and learned of the situation. Zeets was very emotional and cried. My mother was dismayed and upset. She exclaimed that no good ever came from the damned farm.

* * * * * *

A few years later, in early summer, the barn burned to the ground. My father was able to rent a barn down the road to house the cows. My father and brothers started working on building a new barn, and I ended up using my two-week vacation to join them so it would be completed in time to store hay to feed the animals the next winter. Zeets and the children made the best of it. Zeets helped my mother and the kids enjoyed playing with the animals. By the end of the two weeks, the barn was sufficiently completed so that the cows could come back. That was the last time I ever went back to the farm. A few years later, my father retired from the railroad. My parents auctioned off all the equipment and livestock and sold the farm. Richard and Robert were married by then and working factory jobs. My parents and Cathy moved to a small house in Lansing, Michigan, near my sister Dorothy and her family. Finally, after over 30 years, my mother's dream of leaving the farm came true. They were only a few blocks from church and there was a little garden for my father to "farm."

CHAPTER 23
LIFE IN ST. LOUIS

We were so thankful that we had been blessed with two beautiful children. We considered adopting more, but the Supreme Court case, *Roe v. Wade*, that legalized abortion resulted in a severe decrease in adoptable infants. There were a lot of childless couples who wanted children and Catholic Charities was giving them priority over couples who already adopted. Zeets and I really did not want to go to any other agency. We loved the experience of having infants, feeding them, and changing diapers. We were satisfied with the gifts God had already given us. Throughout our marriage, there continued to be more miscarriages, three that happened after we adopted Tina and Tommy. When Tina was 15 and Tommy was 13, we were overjoyed when Zeets became pregnant, and we were finally going to have another child. There are no words to express the despair and pain when we lost that child.

Tina started the first grade at Transfiguration Catholic grade school. That year we enrolled her in the Virginia James Dance Academy. She really enjoyed it the first few years, but then she lost interest and it was a struggle to get her to go. It was a shame because she was very good, but we didn't want to force her to do something she didn't enjoy so we didn't sign her up for a fourth year. However, she was involved in Girl Scouting and really liked that. She was in the pilot program, The Pixies, for girls aged five and six. She went on to be a Brownie, Junior, and Cadette, earning her First-Class Award in the 8th grade. Zeets was involved in all of Tina's scouting activities and was a co-leader every year. They organized fundraisers including a glass and aluminum drive, where they earned enough money for the troop to go to the World's Fair in Knoxville, Tennessee in 1982.

Tina was a dainty, shy girl. She was very sensitive. I had to be careful whenever I scolded her. Her lower lip would quiver and stick out far enough for a bird to perch on. And then the tears would come. She was very much a Daddy's girl. In grade school she started calling me Daddy-O. I enjoyed escorting her to her first formal, a Daddy-Daughter Dance. Although she was shy, she had a way of getting her little brother to be her spokesman.

Daddy-Daughter dance

Tommy was the exact opposite. To Tommy, a stranger was just someone he had not met yet but he intended to meet. He was vibrant, outgoing, and kept no secrets. If the neighbors were curious about anything going on in our household, all they had to do was ask Tommy. Tommy's bedroom was in a state of perpetual chaos, except for the rare occasion where he was ordered to clean it up, or at least find the floor. Tom's idea of tidying up his room involved removing the vent on the heating duct and bulldozing his toys into it. We found out about this system when the new owners hired a company to clean the ducts!

Although each of the children had their own room, Tina would often get up in the night and wander down to our room. If she came to Zeets' side of the bed, she would be sent back to her room. So she started coming to Daddy-O's side and met with greater success. However, she would eventually be sent back to her bed. Next, she enlisted Tommy to be her partner in crime. They would drag their blankets and pillows down the hall and set up camp on the floor on my side of the bed.

* * * * * *

Tommy also attended Transfiguration grade school. He started scouting as a Cub in Kindergarten. Early on his personality attracted the other youngsters to him and he always stood out as a leader. He moved on to Webelos and eventually Boy Scouts. He loved the Rocket and Pine Wood Race Car Derbies. I loved helping him design and fabricate his entries. One year, he even won the Pine Wood Derby.

Even though I had to travel often for work, I was always Tommy's assistant scout master. I enjoyed the camp outs and especially liked taking the boys on their hikes which were usually between 10 and 20 miles long. I was getting to experience what I missed out on in my youth. St. Louis was a great scouting town. There were several trails sanctioned by the scouts and when a boy completed one, he would receive a pie-piece shaped badge to adhere to his "brag" vest. Once the rest of the troop saw a new badge, all the boys would want to earn it, too. Before we attempted long hikes, I took the boys on shorter ones and kept increasing the distance to condition them.

We usually did one hike a month unless there was a campout scheduled. The most memorable hike was the Logging Trail Hike which was 20 miles long through an area where trees were harvested for lumber. I submitted a request to scout headquarters and was granted permission to do the hike one January. We planned for the boys to carry extra shoes and clothing in case of inclement weather as well as a supply of food. One of the dads brought a van to carry all the extra gear and a heater in case any of the boys needed to warm up.

Two days before the hike, there was about 14 inches of snow. Zeets was strongly opposed to us going on the hike and urged me to call it off. However, I felt I had planned for every contingency. I even called scout headquarters for advice on whether to proceed and they saw no reason for us to cancel. I then called the parents of each scout and asked if they wanted their sons to proceed with the hike. Every parent agreed and one parent whose child was a diabetic gave me special instructions about administering the medication he would be carrying with him.

On the morning of the hike, we had the van and two other vehicles staged. Every boy in the troop showed up. The snow was deep, but the van was able to go ahead of the boys. We stopped every few miles for rest and snacks. When we started out, the temperature was a couple of degrees below zero. Everything was going well until we were hiking alongside a stream that was iced over. While we were approaching a bridge, one of the boys decided to cross on the ice instead. Before we could stop him, the ice broke and he fell into freezing waist deep water. We pulled him out and rushed him up the trail to the van his father was driving. He was able to change out of his wet clothes and warm up and complete the entire hike.

With my help and encouragement, Tommy continued earning Merit Badges. He reached Star level before we left St. Louis. By being involved as an assistant scout leader, I got to fulfill my dreams of being a scout that I was denied when I was a boy.

The Scouts' big fundraiser was the monthly newspaper drive. All the scouts and adult leadership were involved. I would drive down the street and Tommy and the other boys would pick up the bundles left at curbside. Often people would come out to bring the papers to the cars. Tommy was so outgoing and gregarious; he would always run up and greet them. We would rendezvous at the scout master's house and off load our papers into a pickup truck. A bunch of the boys would jump in my car and we would follow the truck to the recycling plant to unload. Although it was work, the boys made it into a social event.

Tommy was also very active in sports: football, soccer, baseball, and swimming. I was always an assistant coach for his teams: to shag balls and help in any way I was needed. Just as it was with scouting, I was able to experience the joy of sports that I was deprived of as a boy. After a couple of years of playing soccer on a half field, when Tommy was in the 3rd grade, they started playing on a full field. When they played on the half field, there was never any doubt of the location of the ball. It was always surrounded by a cluster of boys and a cloud of dust— it looked like Pigpen from the Peanuts cartoon. Once they moved up to the full field, it was important to teach them to maintain their positions and learn strategy.

* * * * * * *

During one of the early full field practices, I was standing in the backfield coaching the boys to maintain their positions. The ball was moving toward me. I was focused on the players I was coaching. The boy who was moving the ball was so focused that he didn't see me, he ran into my right leg causing it to bend in an unnatural position, knocking me to the ground. I felt something come loose and move. They took me to the ER and confirmed that I tore the medial collateral ligament of my right knee, the same knee that was injured when a pig attacked and bit me when I was a freshman in high school.

I did a little research and was able to get an appointment with the orthopedic surgeon for the St. Louis Cardinal's football team. The surgery was performed at Barnes Jewish Hospital. It was the late 1970s and arthroscopic surgery had only recently become widespread. I was a case study for several pre-med students and nurses who observed the surgery and interviewed me afterward. The surgery was successful, and my right knee was good for over 30 years until I needed a total knee replacement when I was 70.

* * * * * * *

After I was promoted to GS-12, I applied for several positions and time after time I was not selected even though I was the most qualified. I came to realize the positions were usually wired for a particular person who had a mentor. Since I did not have a mentor, I decided to beef up my resumé. I completed my master's degree in electrical engineering and obtained my professional engineering (PE) license. I was frustrated and discussed it with my friend Bernadette in HR. She told me to hang in there and, sooner or later, I would probably get one of those positions.

A short while later, the Army decided they needed to produce a new scout helicopter with upgraded technology to replace the OH-58. A new program management office was being stood up to pursue the effort. Bernadette contacted me and asked if I would be interested in the position. It would be a temporary GS-13 as part of the Army Helicopter Improvement Program (AHIP). I would be working with a colonel, a major, and a secretary. I was overjoyed because I saw it as a steppingstone to higher rated positions. Our initial task was to draft a proposal for a replacement aircraft. The colonel's main job was briefing Congress and higher headquarters. The major, who was also an engineer, and I worked on the proposal specifications.

The command solicited proposals from helicopter manufacturers, both foreign and domestic, for a new scout helicopter based on our requirements. We received several proposals and narrowed it down to two companies, Bell Helicopter and Hughes Helicopters. Each would produce a prototype for a "fly off" competition. A source selection board was convened and evaluated the performance of the two helicopters. Bell was awarded the contract to produce the OH-58D Kiowa Warrior.

The requirements for the aircraft were four rotor blades instead of two, advanced avionics, and a Mast Mounted Sight (MMS) system comprised of a thermal imaging, television, laser range finder, and designator systems. In addition to its scouting mission, the helicopter needed to have other capabilities, such as field artillery and reconnaissance support. Lastly, it should be able to independently support ground forces with its firepower. It was the first helicopter fitted with a wire strike protection system, a scissor-like device mounted at the front to protect the helicopter from electric, telephone, and other wires that pose a threat when flying at low altitude. After testing the system on the Kiowa Warrior, manufacturers began to use the system on other helicopters as well.

* * * * * * *

While working in AHIP, I received my permanent GS-13 promotion. One of the requirements to work in the AHIP was to take a five-month Program Manager's Course at Fort Belvoir, Virginia, near Washington, D.C. I had been scheduled to attend the previous June, but the colonel requested I postpone it until we had the contract awarded. It was now December and the colonel told me he wanted me to attend the class that started in January. I did not want to go to the course at that time as it would mean leaving Zeets and the children alone for the long St. Louis winter. However, the colonel said he was retiring soon and he wanted to ensure I got into the class because I gave up attending it previously at his request.

I packed up and drove to Virginia right after New Year's Day, 1982. I was assigned accommodations in the Bachelor Officers Quarters (BOQ). The weather in Virginia was brutal that January. The snowy and icy conditions contributed to the horrific crash of Air Florida Flight 90. The aircraft struck the 14th Street Bridge in Washington, D.C, slamming into seven vehicles before plunging into the freezing waters of the Potomac River. Nearly all the passengers and crew as well as several motorists were killed. A few weeks later, on January 30 and 31, back home in St. Louis, there was a once in a century blizzard blanketing the region in 12 to 24 inches of snow. Tommy was in the 6th grade and took over as chief of snow removal in my absence. My colonel kept in contact with Zeets to see if she needed any help, but she assured him everything was under control. She told me she thought he felt guilty that my family was alone.

1982-1990

LEAVING ST. LOUIS

CHAPTER 24
A CHANGE OF ADDRESS

In February, I found a note in my student mailbox to call a colonel at the Army Materiel Command (AMC). The next day during a class break, I returned his call and he offered me a GS-14 engineering position in his office assessing the reliability of Army Aviation. The new position would be at the AMC Headquarters on Eisenhower Road in Alexandria, Virginia. I thanked him for his interest and commended him on his fine choice. I told him I had to consult with my wife before I could make any decision. I also let him know the class I was attending would not be over until the end of May.

That night I called Zeets. Off and on over the years we had discussed moving to the Washington, D.C. area mostly because of the lack of high-grade positions in the St. Louis area. Also, there were rumors swirling around that the Army Aviation command was going to move to Huntsville, Alabama (eventually it did in 1995). Zeets was very supportive of the idea and said, "Let's make the move." She was enthusiastic about the idea of living in the D.C. area and felt that all our relatives would want to come visit us there. The next day I called the colonel, my future supervisor, and accepted the offer.

He wanted me to start right away but I wanted to finish the course. In the end, he agreed I would start in June and they would pay my relocation expenses. I let my current boss know and he was happy for me. I arranged to come back over the next holiday weekend to hand off my assignments and find a realtor to sell the house. Since the house was relatively new and in good condition we wouldn't need to do any work on it before we put it on the market. Unfortunately, the housing market was a nightmare and mortgage interest rates were at an all-time high of over 18%.

At night and on weekends, I met with Metro D.C. area realtors to look for our new home. I would drive from the houses I looked at to my new office to get an idea of my future commute. I had the luxury of time because houses weren't selling in the Metro D.C. area. Zeets arranged for Tina and Tommy to stay with a friend and came to look at the three houses I had honed in on. The house we decided on was in the Mount Vernon area on Parry Lane. The location was close to my new job and many potential future jobs. But best of all, it had an assumable mortgage at the current owner's interest rate. During that week, Zeets looked for schools for Tina, who would be a freshman, and Tommy, who was going into the seventh grade. She registered Tina at St. Mary's Academy and Tommy at St. Louis Catholic grade school in Virginia. Additionally, she registered Tina at St. Thomas Aquinas High School and Tommy at Transfiguration grade school in St. Louis.

To assume the loan on the house required a sizable down payment, which we had, but it was tied up in the equity of the St. Louis house. Zeets and I approached our parents and asked for a short-term loan (with interest, at the current CD rate) but none of them had the ability to do so. I approached my father's sister, my aunt Ann, and she graciously agreed. She was single, never married, and worked for Western Electric. She was very frugal and consequently had a good nest egg saved. We were scheduled to close on the new house when I graduated from my course at the end of May. The only snag was that there was no buyer for our St. Louis home.

CHAPTER 25
LIVING THE BACHELOR LIFE

The end of May 1982 arrived. I graduated from my course and we closed on the house in Alexandria. The house had been a rental for the past few years before we purchased it, therefore, it was in disrepair. It needed a new roof, and to be painted inside and out. Also, all the landscaping would have to be removed and replanted. We now had two mortgages and a sizable loan payment to my aunt. I took two weeks of leave before starting my new position. I brought a frame axle and wheels and built a wooden 8-foot by 4-foot trailer. I drove back to St. Louis to spruce up the house to attract buyers.

Zeets and I had a long discussion about what to do next. Tina and Tommy were constantly fighting with one another and vying for Zeets' affection. Zeets was overwhelmed as Tina's Girl Scout leader, assisting with Tommy's Boy Scout Troop, and shuttling the children to their swim practices and meets. We decided Zeets and Tina would stay in St. Louis and keep up the house until it was sold. Also, they had big plans, Zeets was taking Tina's Girl Scout Troop to the World's Fair the next month. I would take Tommy to Virginia.

* * * * * * *

I loaded up the trailer with all my tools and most of Tommy's belongings. We started out on a Thursday at 8 pm. Traffic was light and we were making good time until we got close to the Indiana-Ohio border when the car's water pump bearing seal failed. I got on my CB radio and found an auto parts store about 15 miles away. It was around midnight. I drove to the next rest area and filled two 5-gallon jugs and topped off the engine cooling system and left the radiator cap off.

My plan was to drive to the auto parts store adding water to the engine along the way. However, about halfway there, the water pump shaft connected to the cooling fan broke and destroyed the radiator. So now I needed a water pump and a radiator. I was able to reach the exit and pulled into the auto parts store parking lot at 4 am. I removed the water pump and radiator and waited for the store to open only to find they didn't have any of the parts I needed. The owner located a water pump at a store a mile away and was going to try to locate a radiator while I walked to the other store to buy the water pump. Tommy was left to guard the car, trailer, and tools.

When I returned, I started installing the new water pump and the store owner informed me that he located a radiator that was going to be delivered. A short while later, a man named Jim, an "Angel," drove up and asked if I needed help. I said everything was under control, but once I got the radiator I was going to need a jump. He agreed to wait around and help me. A short time later, a disheveled young man drove up in a beat-up pickup truck with a rusty mud-covered radiator. I asked him if he checked it for leaks. He didn't respond. He threw the radiator into the back of the pickup truck and drove off. Jim observed all this and came over and told me he knew the young man and that he wasn't trustworthy. I asked Jim if he knew where I could get a new radiator or get mine repaired. He did. He said he would take me there. The owner of the shop told me he could repair it, but he couldn't get to it until Monday. Jim suggested we look for another repair shop.

Jim said he needed to check on his daughter who was home alone and I said I needed to check on Tommy. We broke out the food Zeets had packed for us and a short time later Jim came back with a brand-new radiator. I asked him what I owed him and he said, "Whatever." I installed it and wrote Jim a check for the amount the repairs would have cost and he was pleased with that. He gave me a jump and Tommy and I were on the road again. At dusk, we were approaching the West Virginia border. I heard a weird sound coming from the trailer. I pulled over and saw that the re-tread on one of the tires was coming off. I pulled into a garage and asked if I could borrow a big axle jack. The owner was about to close but said he would stay open to help me. We changed the tire and he would not take any compensation for his services.

* * * * * * *

It was Friday night, and we were back on the road again. I was drinking cokes and coffees to stay awake. I was determined to get to my new home. When we reached the I-495 Beltway, it started to rain heavily. We reached the house but couldn't back the trailer into the garage as it was too high. We had to unload the trailer in the pouring rain before we could get it and the car inside. We spread our blankets out on a bedroom floor and crashed. I had planned to find a pay phone and call Zeets in the morning.

Tommy and I awoke about midday and went to IHOP to get some breakfast. I found a phone and called Zeets. She was frantic. She had called my parents and the police. She even called our new neighbors, Jack and Carol Bobko, whom we had met when we came to look at the house. They did not know Tommy and I had arrived because we pulled into the garage in the middle of the night. I explained the various car and trailer mishaps that delayed our arrival, and we talked about how lucky we were that nothing seriously bad had happened. Tommy and I headed back to the house and were greeted by the Bobkos who told me Zeets was worried about us. We shared the story of our adventures with them and Tommy, being his usual friendly self, ensured that no detail was left out.

That 1969 Chevy Impala with the shiny new replacement radiator would be our car for many years to come. Both Tina and Tom would learn how to drive in that car. When Tommy graduated from college, we traded the Impala in for a new Saturn for him. Two years after we traded the car in, we received a phone call from the Montgomery County Maryland police department informing us that the Impala with our expired plates on it had been parked in front of the headquarters building for months. They wanted to know if we would donate it to be used as a decoy car. We told them we traded it in years ago and as far as we were concerned, they could use it however they wanted. I occasionally think of my "Angel" Jim and wonder if someone is still looking for that beautiful radiator that magically appeared for me.

* * * * * * *

On June 1, 1982, I started working at my new job. Tommy was on summer vacation from school. To keep him out of trouble I gave him a lot of chores to complete each day and strict orders not to leave the house for any reason. After he did his chores, he always found time to open the window of his second-floor bedroom and practically crawl out on the roof. He greeted everyone who passed by and tried to engage them in conversation. Tommy was the friendliest kid you would ever meet.

One of his new "open-window" friends was a retired lady, Mrs. Mullins, who came by with her dog on her daily walk. Soon Mrs. Mullins knew everything about Tommy, me, the house, and his mother and sister back in St. Louis. Mrs. Mullins lived down the street with her daughter's family. Her daughter oversaw the volunteers at the White House. After work, I would come home and do yard work and home repairs getting everything ready for the ladies to join us.

Zeets and I talked every evening on the phone. There was still no movement on selling the St. Louis house. All we could do was hope and pray that things would work out. It wasn't possible to make any plans. Zeets took Tina's Girl Scout troop to the World's Fair in Knoxville that June. Every couple of weeks, Tommy and I would drive the car and trailer back to St. Louis to visit Zeets and Tina. I met with the realtor trying to come up with ideas to make the house more attractive to buyers. I would take care of things around the house and load up more household goods to take to Virginia. One of the options we discussed was to rent the St. Louis house, but we just didn't feel comfortable with the idea.

Zeets and I decided that if the house didn't sell by the end of the summer, Tina would start high school in St. Louis and Tommy would start junior high in Virginia. We continued to pray to Saint Jude for a solution. At the end of July, a man who was transferring to the St. Louis area drove by our house and saw the "For Sale" sign. He asked Zeets if he could see the house. She called the realtor and was told to let him look around. Two days later, his real estate agent contacted ours and he toured the house again. Later that day he made an offer of a substantial down payment; however, he didn't want a bank loan. He wanted us to continue to carry our note, and he would make payments to us until interest rates dropped and he could get a bank loan. Additionally, he wanted possession on the first of August. We reluctantly agreed as he was the only game in town. Zeets and Tina moved to Virginia just in time for the new school year.

* * * * * * *

The day the moving van arrived from St. Louis, before the movers even got it unloaded, my sister Pat and brother-in-law Dave showed up on our doorstep for an unexpected visit. They had been vacationing in the area and decided to come see our new place. Zeets and I soon realized that many of our friends and relatives would probably want to come for a free D.C. vacation. Tommy introduced Zeets to the neighbors, Mrs. Mullins and her daughter. Within two weeks, Zeets had an interim security clearance and was carpooling with three other ladies working as a volunteer in the correspondence section of the White House.

Zeets met so many new friends at her volunteer job, and she quickly learned the lay of the land including where to shop and all the best doctors. She was part of the committee that would see President Reagan off and welcome him home from travel. She said she could see the concern on Nancy's face as she watched Marine One take off from the White House lawn on trips to dangerous destinations. She was invited to White House holiday parties at Christmas and Easter. She was able to add friends and relatives to the Christmas Card list. Her father (a lifelong Democrat) proudly displayed his Christmas card from Ronald Regan on his mantle for years. Because she had beautiful penmanship, she did a lot of the handwritten correspondence. After about two years at the White House, she got a full-time nursing job with Blue Cross/Blue Shield.

* * * * * * *

Zeets knew she had health issues back in St. Louis, but was in denial, referring to her diabetes as "a sugar problem." She made an appointment with one of the best endocrinologists on the East Coast. When I came home from work the evening of her appointment, I found her in tears. She said the doctor wanted to hospitalize her and run tests. She told him she could control things on her own. In St. Louis, she had always been able to talk her doctors into doing things her way. But her new doctor was having none of it. He told her if she was going to be his patient, she would have to follow his recommendations. Zeets checked into the hospital and was put on insulin. She had to stay for several days to have her diet regulated and her blood sugar monitored.

Because of her condition, she began to study everything she could and eventually was certified as a Diabetic Educator. She worked evenings in her new doctor's office teaching patients how to inject themselves with insulin. She even let them practice on her with saline. She worked very hard creating training materials and providing one-on-one instruction.

CHAPTER 26
TINA & TOMMY

When we first moved to Virginia, both children attended Catholic school. However, all the children in the neighborhood attended public school and Tina and Tommy really wanted to go to school with their friends. We lived in the Mount Vernon area of Alexandria with highly rated public schools. We agreed that they could go to 10th and 8th grade in public school, but they would have to take a college prep curriculum. Additionally, we required them to participate in at least one sport and they both chose swimming.

Tommy continued working on Merit Badges and the requirements to earn his Eagle Scout. Even though I had to travel a bit more for work, I continued to be an assistant scout master. I really enjoyed going on the campouts and hikes, as well as working with Tommy on his Eagle Project. Tommy organized and led the painting of the newly constructed animal enclosures at Oxon Hill Farm, a part of the National Park Service in Maryland. After he received his Eagle he was invited to join the Order of the Arrow which he thoroughly enjoyed.

Tommy as a Boy Scout

God had blessed Zeets and I with two gifted children. We encouraged them to develop their social skills and work ethic and to get good grades. Tina and Tommy each had their own *Washington Post* paper route. Every morning around 5 am Zeets and I would get up with the children. The various parts of the paper were delivered to our driveway and we would assemble them. We would drop the bundles off at the corner of each block and the children would distribute them. At the end of each month, they would collect the payments from the subscribers. Out of those payments, they had to pay the regional distributor for the papers. The remainder, including tips, was theirs to keep. There were times, like at Christmas, when tips were very good. We set up a college savings account for each of the children, but they were allowed to keep a small portion for their personal spending. After one year of delivery, Tina was named the *Washington Post* "Carrier of the Year." Soon thereafter, Tina decided to give up her route and Tommy agreed to take it on. Although he never became an award winner, he developed personal relationships with his customers, and they hired him for odd jobs.

*　*　*　*　*　*　*

I was still working at AMC conducting reliability evaluations of systems under development. The work was fine, but my heart was not in it. I wanted to be managing programs. A promotion opportunity arose for a position in a highly classified Special Operations Aviation program with The Night Stalkers at Fort Belvoir. I began to think about the Senior Executive Service (SES), the classification for non-competitive senior leadership positions, filled by career employees or political appointees. I felt another advanced degree would increase my chances so I began an online program for a doctorate in Mechanical Engineering. Many of the graduate courses I had previously taken were accepted into my degree program. I utilized the technical information I acquired in developing the Electro-Mechanical Method of Measuring the Contour of Helicopter Rotor Blades for my dissertation. I completed my doctorate degree in 1995.

CHAPTER 27
BOATING

For the first few years we were in Northern Virginia, I heard endless stories from the guys in the office about their boats. Some had sail boats, other power boats, but all agreed the area was wonderful for watercraft. Zeets and I discussed the pros and cons of sailing versus power boating. We agreed on several features we wanted in a boat and concluded that a power boat would be best.

We wanted a boat large enough to stay on for weekends where we could comfortably sleep, eat, and relax. Additionally, we had no interest in trailering the boat and hauling it in and out of the water every time we wanted to use it. Because I am an engineer, I wanted to plan for all contingencies, so we decided on a twin-engine boat. Now the hunt for the right vessel was on. We combed the classified ads, visited boat dealers, and drove around exploring the various marinas in the Chesapeake Bay area. Initially, Zeets accompanied me, but she quickly grew weary of the search. She told me I was on my own and when I found the boat I wanted she would come and look at it.

Our budget restricted the hunt to somewhat older boats. Unfortunately, these vessels needed lots of repairs and the owners would say anything to try to sell them. Each time I found one I was interested in, my surveyor would point out numerous deficiencies that the seller had not disclosed. Therefore, I started looking at newer used boats. One Sunday, I saw an ad in the paper for a two-year-old, 28-foot Bayliner cabin cruiser with twin engines. It was docked in Deale, Maryland at a marina about an hour from our house. I went to check it out. Deale was a quaint marina town and the boat was in excellent shape. The couple who owned it were getting divorced, therefore, the slip was available too. It was priced a little above what we hoped to pay, but it met all our other criteria, so Zeets said: "Let's just do it!"

We made a contract contingent on a sea trial and a marine survey inspection. Everything checked out beautifully, but during the sea trial, I was a little intimidated. Wanting a boat and driving a boat are two very different things. Suddenly, two engines and 28 feet seemed like a lot to handle. However, we closed the deal and got the keys on a Friday. Bright and early Saturday morning, we packed a few things and the whole family headed off to the boat.

There was some fuel in the tank so we decided to take a short ride out into the bay. On the way out of the marina, there was a fair amount of boat traffic and it appeared to be total chaos. I didn't know the rules of the "road" but it didn't seem like anyone else did either. I was amazed that there weren't endless accidents. We just made it to the bay when I turned around and headed back. When we returned to the marina, there were plenty of other boaters to help us get back into our slip. My conversations with others at the marina were guarded as I was afraid of sounding stupid as a first-time boater. Zeets and I agreed to take a boating safety course. Even if those around us didn't know the rules, I wanted to know them. The next week we found a Coast Guard Auxiliary Flotilla in Maryland and started a boating safety course. The class was free; we only needed to purchase the textbook for our homework assignments.

The boat provided weekend recreation for our family and friends. We loved the camaraderie among the boating crowd. There were old salts with a lot of sea stories and much of what they said contradicted the instruction we had been receiving in our boating safety course. But they were great folks who were pleasant to be around and they taught me a lot. Every Saturday night we had a marina-wide cookout and potluck. Even if the weather was foul, there was overhead protection at the Scuttlebutt Marina and, rain or shine, we spent entire weekends on the boat. We had all the creature comforts like heating, air conditioning, a shower, toilet, kitchen, and TV. The boat also provided many peaceful hours for me to write my dissertation.

The six-week boating safety class was proving to be beneficial and I was soaking up information like a sponge. Additionally, I practiced maneuvering and docking in the calm backwaters of the bay. I felt reasonably confident in my ability to handle the *Tina Marie*. Soon after we got the boat, a marina across the bay was having a family fun fair and concert. We decided to take the boat there for the weekend. We made reservations and a friend of Tina's joined us. When we went over early Saturday morning, the weather was fine and the bay was calm. We tied up in our assigned slip and began to enjoy the festivities. The children windsurfed and played beach volleyball. Our plan was to spend the night, but the children were restless to return home. I agreed to head back to our marina in Deale.

We started back but once we got out into the bay, the water began to get rough. We discussed turning back, but it didn't seem that bad, so we continued homeward. About halfway back, things took a turn. Now there was no turning back. I remembered what they taught in the safety course and the pictures in the textbook on how to navigate such sea conditions flashed into my mind. I needed to climb each wave at a 45-degree angle and reduce my speed while descending so that the bow would not dig into the oncoming wave. Zeets took the children into the cabin: they put on their PFDS and huddled in the lowest point, the galley floor. The refrigerator door flew open and the contents spewed all over them. Lesson Number 1: Lash all doors in inclement weather! Zeets broke out the beads and immediately started praying the Rosary with the children.

I was alone on the fly bridge taking one wave at a time. The first time I violated the 45-degree angle rule up on the crest of the wave, the bow slammed down roughly. When I was in the trough, I could barely see over the top of the oncoming wave. Fortunately, I was able to reduce the engine speed, control the boat, and avert catastrophe. Every seventh wave was of an increasing height. Eventually, I was looking at a wall of water rushing toward me. Lesson Number 2: Don't disregard the 45-degree angle rule! That perfect storm was my Baptism as a Captain.

Zeets yelled out that Tommy was not feeling well and he was coming up on the fly bridge to be with me. He sat on the bench behind me and asked if we were going to be okay. I told him we would. Although the sea was rough, the boat was handling it. After a few minutes of silence, I looked back and he was sound asleep. I guess he only needed a little reassurance from his dad, the novice captain. I continued working one wave at a time and we finally approached the inlet waterway to our marina. It was very sheltered and when we entered, it was like floating on a lily pond.

People ran over to help us tie up at our dock. They were surprised we had been out as the weather report said the bay was very rough that day. We totally agreed with those old salts. The trip out had taken about 45 minutes. The return trip took over two hours. Once on the dock, Zeets put her hands on her hips and loudly announced that her half of the boat was for sale! I had a different reaction to the experience. I felt very good about the way the boat performed and how I handled it. I was determined more than ever to take advantage of additional Coast Guard Auxiliary training. That evening on the 10 pm news, the weatherman reported that the Chesapeake Bay showed its ugly self with 30-foot waves.

* * * * * * *

The Auxiliary offered several specialty classes to its members who met the prerequisites such as navigation, weather, and seamanship. There was a flotilla that met at the Mount Vernon Yacht Club near our house. They were happy to have us because we owned a boat. We joined not only for the classes, but for the social aspect. The very first specialty course we took was about weather.

At the time, there was almost no commercial assistance available to boaters in need of help such as towing or if the craft was taking on water. The only help boaters could get was from the Coast Guard or the Auxiliary. The "Good Samaritan" aspect of the Auxiliary appealed to me. I felt my boat and I could be of service to fellow boaters in need. Of course, to begin with, I needed additional training and to acquire some specialized equipment. Zeets and I started training to become crew-qualified and procured equipment like a tow line, a megaphone, and PFDs. We had to log many hours and demonstrate proficiencies before being granted our coxswain ratings. It took a couple of years and then we were eligible to receive official government orders from the Coast Guard to conduct safety patrols.

Additionally, I became qualified as a Courtesy Marine Examiner to inspect boats for safety compliance. Our findings and recommendations were confidential between the Auxiliary and the boat owners. I got permission from the Fort Washington, Maryland marina to set up a boating safety inspection booth on the weekends. In two years, I inspected over 1000 boats. In addition to providing a service to the public, I was learning about all kinds of boats in the process and gathering lots of tips and techniques. Zeets and I began teaching boating safety classes. Back when I worked with the Boy Scouts, I learned to tie dozens of different knots and I demonstrated them during class.

After a couple of years, I was elected Vice Commander of the Mount Vernon Coast Guard Auxiliary Flotilla. And a few years later, I was elected Flotilla Commander. I met a private aircraft pilot with a plane who was instructor qualified and explained our mission. I convinced him to join the Auxiliary. He encouraged two fellow pilots with planes of their own to join. All three aircraft were certified to conduct search and rescue missions. Under my leadership, we now had an air wing.

I was encouraged to move up the ranks to become a Vice Division Captain. However, I was really enjoying myself at the Flotilla level and declined. The other reason I declined was that I had been bitten by the "Big Boat Bug." Zeets and I thought that if we were having so much fun with a 28-foot boat, how much more fun would it be to have a 38-foot boat. We eventually purchased a 38-foot cabin cruiser with two state rooms, twin diesel engines, air conditioning, an ice maker, and entertainment center. We christened her the *Tina Marie II*. The Big Boat Bug did not stop biting there. Next came *Tom's Toy*. Eventually, we wound up with a 47-foot Mainship with 3 state rooms each with a TV, twin diesel engines, five air/heat units, auto pilot, radar, and two heads with showers: the *Tom's Toy II*.

Our retirement goal for *Tom's Toy II* was offshore long-range cruising. However, before retirement it provided a terrific platform for the children and grandchildren to enjoy cruising throughout the Chesapeake Bay and its tributaries. Along the way, I earned a 100-ton Merchant Marine license. This allowed me to be a commercial captain and opened the door to many post-retirement opportunities. I remained active in the Auxiliary for over 35 years and am still a member today.

CHAPTER 28
THE LATE 80s

In 1985, three years after we moved to Alexandria, I received a promotion to GS-15 with a handsome salary increase. My new job was to evaluate the performance of Army weapon systems under development. I made recommendations to the decision makers about whether to fund the systems into production. Zeets was still employed by Blue Cross/Blue Sheild as a utilization review nurse for all the hospitals in the DC Metro area. She was also the chairperson of the benefits appeals board. The buyer of our house back in St. Louis found it to his advantage to refinance the house and we were finally out from under that loan. I was then able to repay my aunt in full the money she advanced us.

Zeets and I were now in a financial position to restart the investment program we began back in St. Louis. We purchased stocks and mutual funds and added to the children's college accounts. I established budgets for future household expenses and to purchase a new car. We started out in our marriage by paying all our credit cards bills in full upon receipt and continued that practice. My philosophy was to never finance anything unless it was necessary. Therefore, we never made purchases we couldn't afford. Rather, we saved for things. We also made extra mortgage payments as often as possible. Early on we set up accounts for retirement and emergency funds. Finally, we found ourselves in a comfortable position financially.

* * * * * *

Tina graduated from high school in June 1986. She was torn between pursuing a Chemical Engineering degree at the University of Virginia (UVA) in Charlottesville or accepting a full scholarship into the pre-pharmacy program at Virginia Commonwealth University (VCU) in Richmond. She had been offered on-campus housing on the honors floor with guaranteed acceptance into the College of Pharmacy if she kept a B average. I would have loved to make that decision for her, but it was her career, and she had worked hard to achieve the high grades to afford her the choices. On the day of the decision deadline, she and Zeets headed to the post office with two envelopes. One contained the acceptance letter and a check to UVA; the other contained an acceptance of the VCU offer. She dropped the letter to Charlottesville in the mail.

However, in her sophomore year she had second thoughts about being a Chemical Engineer and met with the Assistant Dean of the VCU Pharmacy School about a possible transfer into the pharmacy program. Her grades were fine, but she would need to complete a summer program of two semesters of Organic Chemistry and labs. That was a very stressful summer, but my Tina succeeded. She started the pharmacy program in September 1988 - but unfortunately, without the full-ride scholarship.

* * * * * * *

In 1988, two other significant events occurred. On April 10, 1988, my mother called to tell me that my father had been killed in an automobile accident the day before. He was 72 years old. This was extremely depressing for me. I had always hoped that one day he would congratulate me on my accomplishments and tell me he was proud of my efforts at school and my career. But now that would never take place. I began to think that maybe I should have done more to foster our relationship as adults. But every time I took my family home to visit my parents, he would find fault with things I said and did. A few days after his death, my family and I attended his funeral. My mother was extremely distraught; this tragedy occurred two months before their 50th wedding anniversary. They had been planning a big celebration.

* * * * * * *

The second major event was that Tommy embarked on his BA degree in the Computer Science program at Old Dominion University (ODU) in Norfolk, Virginia. His entry into college life was rather straight-forward, with one exception. Zeets and I set up a bank account for him just as we had for Tina when she started college. There was enough money for discretionary spending given that his tuition, room and board, and books were paid in full. At the end of her first semester, Tina had only spent a few dollars and didn't need anything.

That was not the case with Tommy. About six weeks into his first semester he called home and requested that we add more money into his account. That request required an "audit" of his expenditures to date. He revealed that he didn't care for the food provided by his meal plan and he was going out to eat a lot. Also, he was the Big Man on Campus purchasing pizzas for many of his dorm buddies. We had to inform him— again— that the amount we put in his account was meant to last the entire semester. All his expenses were paid in full including his 7-day-a-week meal plan. Therefore, he was not going to starve, he would just have to adjust his lifestyle. We told him we would refill the account for his second semester. However, over his Christmas break we learned that Tommy Joe was selling blood to fund his discretionary spending. Zeets and I were extremely sad about it, but we felt he needed to learn how to manage his money. Evidently, that Boy Scout Merit Badge on Personal Finances and Budgeting and his paper route business did not accomplish all we had hoped.

During the summer, he returned home to Northern Virginia and was re-hired into the Summer Student Employment Program with the Department of the Army Material Command that he had worked for during high school. He worked on IT problems. Upon graduation four and a half years later, the Army Material Command requested that their IT support contractor hire him.

* * * * * * *

On April 26, 1989, Zeets' father died. He was 99 years old and had been married for 65 years. He had been a very good friend and father-in-law and I truly missed him. Zeets' mom was 86 years old at the time and suffering from late-stage cancer. That year, she spent several months with us including the Christmas holidays. After that, she spent several weeks with each of her remaining children before her death on June 18, 1990.

* * * * * * *

In December 1989, I was hired as the Chief Engineer supporting the Army Special Operational Forces, a top-secret clandestine unit. I designed and oversaw the fabrication of specialized hardware to support the 160th Special Operations Aviation Regiment, The Night Stalkers. I was on call and tied to a pager 24/7. This was a very interesting job, but I still had my sights set on potential positions as a Senior Executive Service (SES) employee. To enhance my potential to bring that to fruition, I finished my dissertation and earned my PhD in Mechanical Engineering from LaSalle University.

* * * * * * *

In 1996, I also applied and was accepted into a nine-month senior level master's program at the National Defense University in Washington, D.C. at the Industrial College of the Armed Forces. In June 1997, I was awarded a Master of Science in National Resource Strategy and Program Management. It was the Department of Defense policy that upon completion of a senior level program, a candidate would not return to his or her previous job but would be assigned to a new position. Therefore, I was reassigned to be the Deputy Director of System Engineering at the Ballistic Missile Defense Organization on President Reagan's Strategic Defense Initiative known as "Star Wars."

Star Wars was a program to develop a defense shield over the entire United States of America and ultimately its allies, to prevent a missile attack. To accomplish this engineering challenge, I managed five divisions of 276 government employees and contractor support personnel. I was responsible for a multi-million-dollar budget to develop and test its feasibility. This program was the goal of my dreams. This was not a 40 hour a week job— it was pure enjoyment. It was fun. I had a large corner office, security, my name on the door, and the personnel and budget responsibility accordingly. The goal of moving into an SES position was no longer a priority and I ceased to pursue it.

1991-2013

The Empty Nest

CHAPTER 29
TINA'S GRADUATION AND MARRIAGE

Tina graduated from VCU School of Pharmacy in 1991 and began working as a pharmacist. She shared a house in Alexandria with three other women. Two years later, on October 30, 1993, she married Earl, her pharmacy school classmate from Marion, Virginia. Instead of the elaborate wedding Zeets was planning, I suggested I purchase an aluminum ladder and let them elope and use the money to get their first house. Zeets was adamantly against that suggestion telling me that she had only one daughter and she was going to have a beautiful wedding for her. With Tina's support and involvement, she did just that.

It was a church wedding with bridesmaids and groomsmen and over 250 guests. Before the ceremony began, the priest asked Earl if he would ever consider becoming a Catholic. He admitted he had not but said: "If that Pope job ever opens up, I'm considering applying for it." Much to everyone's amusement, the priest mentioned it in his homily. Unfortunately, it was pouring rain and the outdoor cocktail hour we planned was moved to the hotel lobby. We had a sit-down dinner and reception. Tina and Earl's favorites, Mickey and Minnie Mouse, adorned the top of their wedding cake. Zeets and I stayed in a suite at the hotel where the reception was held in Old Town Alexandria. The next morning, we had a Continental breakfast in our suite. Everyone showed up with half-open or blood-shot eyes, many in bathrobes, to continue the celebration.

My responsibilities included ensuring that two bars at the reception were adequately stocked and manned and that I sold enough stocks and bonds to fund the entire event. My biggest job and greatest joy was walking my beautiful baby girl down the aisle. This was the finest party Zeets and I had ever given and I think everyone enjoyed it. Earl is the oldest of three boys and his father Danny was a pharmacist and owner of two independent pharmacies. Earl's family has been in Southwest Virginia for generations. They are delightful, loving, and caring people. It was so wonderful to unite our families.

Tom walking Tina down the aisle

Tina and Earl were both employed as pharmacists in Abingdon, Virginia. Tina at The Medicine Shop and Earl at one of his father's pharmacies, Super K. Their family began with their first born, a son, Carter Daniel, on November 1, 1998. He was our very first grandchild, and only grandson. Megan Elizabeth was born on July 31, 2002. Tina and her family lived in Abingdon, a five-and-a-half-hour drive from our Mount Vernon home. Visits back and forth were frequent and enjoyable. When they came to visit us in the summers, we would always go boating.

CHAPTER 30
CANCER

In my late 40s, I developed urinary tract issues. Zeets was a nurse and had many contacts in the medical community and she found a urology surgeon with an outstanding reputation. At my appointment he conducted an exam and ran several tests and treated me for a urinary tract infection with antibiotics. However, the results of the Prostate-Specific Antigen (PSA) test revealed a slightly higher than normal reading. That meant I was in a watch and wait position with repeated tests and exams every six months. After a few years, the exams revealed nothing abnormal, and my PSA results remained unchanged. My doctor surmised that like many men I may just have a slightly elevated PSA but he wanted to continue to monitor me annually.

When I was 55, things changed, my PSA results were dramatically worse. The doctor conducted a biopsy. When Zeets and I met him to get the results he politely informed us that I had prostate cancer. My reaction was blunt, I said "Are you shitting me?" He assured me that he was not and told us that every sample taken from the right side of my prostate was positive for cancer. The good news was that the cancer was completely contained in my prostate and had not metastasized.

The doctor explained all my treatment options and advised me that the one that offered the best outcome was surgery. He told us there was no urgency and that we should go home and talk about it as well as researching my options. The next day, Zeets went to the library and got several books. We read about the pros and cons of the various treatment options. One book in particular *The Prostate: A Guide for Men and the Women Who Love Them* written by Patrick C. Walsh, MD, went into detail about the surgical procedure. After reading it, I joked with Zeets that if I could stay conscious during the operation, I had enough information to perform the procedure myself. I got a second opinion from a specialist at Johns Hopkins, Dr. Walsh, the man who wrote the book, and he confirmed the diagnosis and recommended surgery.

Zeets and I prayed about it. It was a comfort to have such an understanding and supportive wife. We met with the doctor and scheduled the surgery. I reaffirmed that my priority was to remove the cancer and save as much of the nerve as possible and he agreed. I began banking blood for the upcoming procedure. The surgery went as planned and the doctor took several samples to send to pathology to ensure the cancer was completely removed. Once pathology confirmed that was the case, he recommended not to start chemotherapy or radiation right away but rather to monitor me and start it if it was needed. The cancer never came back.

About five years later, Zeets was diagnosed with bladder cancer. Luckily, it was caught early and easily treated with medication rather than surgery. The treatments were administered over a period of several months. The results were positive, and her cancer never returned.

CHAPTER 31
TOMMY'S GRADUATION AND MARRIAGE

In 1997, Tommy graduated college and was employed as an Information Technology Computer Science Specialist. He was engaged to Daniella, affectionately known as Danny. On May 24, 1997, they were married at Good Shepherd Catholic Church in Alexandria, Virginia. It was a beautiful ceremony and reception. However, Zeets and I were only allowed to invite one guest, Tommy's paternal grandmother. There was a lot of discussion about the unfairness of the situation and the fact that his grandmother was elderly and unable to drive. Additionally, she was the sole caretaker of my sister Cathy who had Down Syndrome. Therefore, we were finally allowed to invite Cathy, my sister Dorothy and brother-in-law Ed, and their daughter Cindy, who provided the transportation for the group from Michigan. This was very distressing for us. We had so many friends and relatives who wanted to be included and felt slighted. It was especially hurtful since there were hundreds of guests on the bride's side including mere acquaintances and business colleagues of her father. However, we had no choice but to accept the situation. No other uncles or aunts, including Tommy's Godmother, my sister Mary, were invited.

Danny was the older of two children, with a younger brother Ricky. Her father was the Brazilian representative to the Office of American States in Washington, D.C. Her mother Regina was a homemaker. A second wedding reception was scheduled to take place in Brazil and we were told we would be invited along with several of our close friends. However, when the time came, we were shut out again. The relationship with Danny's family was cordial, but nothing like the loving family feeling we had with Earl's family. It really hurt Zeets very much. She was such a caring and sensitive person and her family was her greatest joy.

Tommy's wedding

Tommy and Danny had their first child, Julia, on March 31, 1999, four months after Carter was born. Their second child, another daughter, Isabela, was born November 15, 2002, four months after Megan was born. These two granddaughters were absolute delights for us. We loved every moment we were able to spend with them. Tommy was very accommodating in sharing his children with us. Danny, on the other hand, was guarded and restricted our access to the girls. Danny seldom visited our home, and when Zeets and I would visit their home, she was always rude to us. When we would arrive at the arranged time, often she would not be there or would not show up for hours. Sometimes she would stay upstairs in her bedroom and wouldn't even come down to greet us until we had already been there for hours. Tommy was always a lovely son and did his best to be a gracious host.

One time, Tina, Earl, Tommy, Danny, Zeets, and I were discussing some trivial matter. Danny was not getting the outcome she sought, and she threatened Zeets and I saying we would never see our granddaughters again! Earl immediately inserted himself and told her that she could not keep her children from their grandparents— it was just wrong. On many occasions after visiting them, Zeets would cry all the way home. When I tried to console her, all I could think to say is that we needed to tolerate the circumstances for Tommy and the girls' sake.

Danny did not like our home and refused to come on many occasions. She did manage to come once or twice a year, on either Christmas or Easter, and those were very lovely times with the grandchildren. We would exchange gifts or hunt for eggs (that Zeets and Tommy took great pains to hide). Once I asked Tommy why Danny didn't want to visit our home. My intent was to rectify whatever the problem might be. He told me that she was not "comfortable," and he did not elaborate any further. I did not push for an explanation. Thankfully, there was one activity that Tommy's entire family enjoyed doing with us— going out on the boats. We did that as frequently as we possibly could.

CHAPTER 32
BUDDY CLUB

Zeets and I thoroughly loved and enjoyed our grandchildren. Whenever possible we would visit them or have them to our home. On the rare occasions when both families were spending the weekend at our house, the four grandchildren and I (aka "Gramps") would have a sleepover in our family room. Air mattresses covered the floor from wall-to-wall for the kids while I slept on the couch. I would tell them stories about their parents, Tina and Tommy, when they were their ages. The stories they enjoyed the most and asked to be retold were of our visits to my parents' farm. The one they loved the best was about Peaches, the calf. The stories would continue until I could hear deep breathing and assumed all four children were asleep. I would stop only to be made aware that one or more of them were still awake and wanted more stories. I would keep going and never ran out of stories. I dubbed our little group "The Buddy Club."

The Buddy Club

One time, The Buddy Club put on a skit for their parents' enjoyment. After they rehearsed, they walked into the living room where the audience was seated and announced the performance: "Sleepover at Gramps!" The four Buddies and I laid on the floor on our right sides in a row starting with the youngest, Isa, to the oldest, me. We were covered with a large blanket and pretended to be asleep. Isa asked Megan, "Is it time yet?" That question would be passed along the line until it reached me. I would then reply to Carter, "Not yet." He would repeat it to Julia, and she passed it on to Megan and Megan told Isa. After a silence of a minute or two, Isa would start the process again. After the third iteration, I responded, "Yes, it is time." And with that the entire Buddy Club rolled over to the left side! The grandchildren and I have always shared fantastic and close relationships.

* * * * * * *

In 2014, the Buddies were reaching ages (between 11 and 14 years old) where I thought learning about investments and finances were appropriate. After consulting with their parents and obtaining approval, I initiated the Buddy Investment Club. This club not only taught the grandchildren how to save and invest money, but it became a mechanism for keeping them connected to one another. The club had a few rules that could not be altered or violated. First, I would provide each grandchild with a sum of money. The money could only be used for investing. No other funds could be added to the funds I provided. Each child was encouraged to get advice and counsel from other people or organizations.

Lastly, if a Buddy removed any money from his or her account, they were out of the club.

Every six months, we would meet to review and discuss the status of the investments. The Buddy with the greatest return on investment would receive a cash award which was a gift, and it could be spent on anything except investment into the Buddy Club account. Every six months, I would add to their accounts again. Initially, the Buddy Investment Club met at my home. However, as the grandchildren grew older and left for college, the meetings were conducted telephonically. Their investments grew and so did their love for one another.

CHAPTER 33
THE YACHT

When we purchased our 47-foot Mainship Cabin Cruiser, christened the *Tom's Toy II*, our intent was to use her for long range cruising in the Caribbean after our retirement. However, before that retirement came, we spent a great many days and nights on board that comfortable yacht. Boats are traditionally given feminine names, and TT2 was certainly an elegant lady. She had a salon with TV, VCR, beautiful furnishings, and a well-stocked wet bar. The couch converted into a double bed when needed. The salon had a dedicated heating/air-conditioner to keep our guests comfortable in all weather conditions. The galley was equipped with a full-sized refrigerator/freezer which Zeets always kept full. It also had an oven, stove, microwave, hot and cold running water, trash compactor, washer, and dryer. The dinette sat six comfortably and had its own heat/AC to keep Zeets, the galley chef, comfortable. Zeets loved to cook and make exotic dishes and specialty cocktails, including her favorite, the Toasted Almond.

She had three staterooms that accommodated two guests each. There were two bathrooms with bathtubs and showers. Each stateroom had its own TV, VCR, and closet. The largest aft stateroom was the Captain's Quarters. The smallest stateroom was located midship. It had a desk and couch which converted into bunk beds. The grandchildren made it into their private little Shangri-La! They used blankets to make the lower bunk a fort. They also loved to snuggle up in the upper bunk, their pretend treehouse and watch cartoons and the movie "George of the Jungle" over and over. The enclosed fly bridge contained all the electronic equipment to navigate the cruiser. There were two radars for detecting weather and boat traffic, a Global Positioning System, a chart plotter, auto-pilot, and three marine radios. The entire boat was wired for public address and music.

Down below deck were two Detroit Diesel 671TI engines, each with 485 horsepower and the capability to cruise at a very comfortable speed. Also in the engine room was a large 12KW diesel generator to provide electrical power to the five heat/AC units and all devices. The generator allowed us to anchor away from a marina. She carried 600 gallons of diesel fuel, 240 gallons of fresh water, and had the capability to hold 200 gallons of wastewater.

Tom's Toy II

Every year after the end of the high boating season, Zeets and I would take a seven-to-ten-day vacation and cruise different sections of the Chesapeake Bay. We enjoyed the natural splendor of the bay without the hustle and bustle of the huge crowds while most of the boating amenities were still open. We took our bicycles with us to explore each town or marina where we docked. We visited museums and Zeets' favorite, gift shops. We enjoyed the local dining and entertainment. Our children and their families were never able to accompany us for the entire duration of these trips but would occasionally meet up with us for a few days.

With time, Zeets' diabetes progressively worsened and our cruising was confined to short trips. If overnight stays were planned, we would be sure to stay at a marina with easy access to ambulance service and an emergency room. Our initial plan for long-range cruising and visiting locations like the Bahamas had to be discarded, but we still enjoyed what we could do and all the socializing at the Mount Vernon Yacht Club.

CHAPTER 34
KNIGHTS OF COLUMBUS

Because I am a Catholic man, for many years, the one group I thought of joining was the Knights of Columbus (KCs). Once the children were married, I finally decided to take the plunge and joined the KCs. In October 2011, after several years of being a Third Degree Knight, I received my Fourth Degree, which is the highest level. My Uncle Jim was the only man in my family to attain Fourth Degree up to that point. However, most of the men in Zeets' family were Fourth Degree Knights. At the time of his death, Zeets' father was the oldest living Fourth Degree KC in the state of Missouri. Zeets was very sick at the time of my Fourth Degree induction, but she put on a brave face and accompanied me to the ceremony and dinner/dance reception to follow.

As a KC, I was very active in my Mount Vernon Council in Northern Virginia. Most every Wednesday and Friday, I worked at the Bingo at our KC hall. I sold raffle tickets, checked winners' cards for accuracy, delivered the cash prizes, and delivered food to the players from the "gourmet" cafe. Many times, Zeets would accompany me and play multiple Bingo cards and partake in the cafe delights. The cafe served hot dogs, hamburgers, soft drinks, and desserts, all prepared by the Knights and their ladies.

Once a month, the students from the culinary class at the local high school would prepare a special meal as part of their classroom assignment. They made about 50 servings of things like stuffed green peppers and meatloaf to sell to the players. These specials sold out immediately and were a big hit with the patrons. Often as players showed up to purchase their Bingo cards, they would ask what the special was and put in their orders.

There were a host of other KC activities that Zeets and I were involved with such as parades, jazz parties, March for Life, and the preparation and distribution of Thanksgiving food baskets to the needy. We also hosted a monthly Pancake Breakfast at our church, Good Shepherd. Zeets would always volunteer with the other wives to help serve. She was very proud of my being a Knight.

All the fundraising events resulted in sizable revenue that was donated to various charitable causes. Working at events earned points or credits which equated to dollars that I could donate to my favorite charity. I selected to donate them to Christ the King Catholic Church (CTK) in Abingdon, Virginia. When I permanently moved to Abingdon, I transferred my Knighthood to the CTK council. I continue to be active at my new church, especially with our big annual fundraiser, the golf tournament.

During the Covid-19 pandemic, the golf tournament and other fundraisers were cancelled. We were very short of funds and in danger of not being able to provide a scholarship to a high school graduate for college. I stepped up and offered the KCs a solution. I donated dozens of my woodworking efforts to be sold after Masses to parishioners and the funds were able to keep the scholarship program afloat.

* * * * * * *

One Sunday after the CTK quarterly pancake breakfast, a young man named Daniel approached me with a request. Daniel always worked in the kitchen with his dad Roby and Chef Robert preparing the food for almost every church event. He asked me to be his Confirmation sponsor. My heart overflowed with joy. It brought tears to my eyes remembering my beloved Gramps, Albert Bartik, who had been my sponsor. I secretly hoped Daniel would choose Thomas as his Confirmation name as I had chosen Albert as mine. He did not, but I was honored to stand up with him as he took his next step in his faith journey.

CHAPTER 35
LIFE IN ABINGDON

Tina and Earl were gainfully employed as pharmacists in Abingdon. Carter and Megan were involved in school and sports. With the decrease in boating activities, Zeets and I found ourselves making the 5 ½ hour trip from Mount Vernon to Abingdon more frequently. After a few years, we considered Abingdon as a retirement location. It would allow us to be close to Tina's family and able to participate in the grandchildren's school, Scouts, and sports activities.

Since we still enjoyed boating, having a retirement home on the water was a priority. After about two years of searching, in 2009, we purchased a home on South Holston Lake less than a mile from Tina and Earl's home. The property also had another building with an apartment, a three-car garage with a grease pit, and a heated workshop that would be ideal for future hobbies. The house was a basic two bedroom, two-and-a-half bath ranch, with a partially finished walk-out basement. We would be able to live entirely on one level. The halls and doorways were very wide, and we commented that they would be able to accommodate future two-way wheelchair traffic. There was only one step to the entrance of the house which was ideal for an aging couple. We began purchasing some furniture and relocating spare items from our Alexandria home. We were spending more leisure time at the lake house than at our boat docked at the Mount Vernon Yacht Club. Much of our lake house time was spent with Tina, Earl, and our two precious grand babies, Carter and Megan.

* * * * * *

In 2010, a political decision was made to move the Missile Defense Program to Huntsville, Alabama. I was strongly encouraged to move with the program with the indication that there would be a promotion to SES. However, if I decided not to move, a position would be found for me in the Metro D.C. area. At that time, Zeets was under the care of many medical specialists in Northern Virginia because of her increasingly worsening diabetic issues. The prospect of relocating and having to find a new set of doctors was daunting.

I declined to relocate and shortly thereafter, I was offered an engineering position at Fort Belvoir with the Army Support Division. The job was located only three miles from our Alexandria home with a beautiful scenic commute along the Potomac River on the George Washington Parkway. A year into the new job, I developed complications in both knees necessitating a total right knee replacement. The plan was to replace my left knee as soon as rehabilitative therapy from the first surgery was completed. While I was still recovering from the first surgery, Zeets slipped into her third and final coma.

Although the doctors did countless tests, they were never able to identify the cause of the first two comas. They considered the third coma to be more severe than the previous ones. I cancelled the scheduled left knee replacement surgery. Thankfully, the problems I had with it were dissipating along with the therapy I was receiving. My attention was now totally devoted to Zeets' medical condition. After several days, she pulled out of the coma, but began a long hospitalization followed by several months in a rehabilitation center for physical, occupational, and speech therapy.

Every day on my way home from work, I went to the rehab center to have dinner with Zeets and spent all day on the weekends with her. After a while, the facility would allow me to take her out for brief periods of time. Her absolute favorite "field trip" was weekend breakfast at IHOP. As part of her occupational therapy, she had to demonstrate that she could complete a household chore. She chose to make breakfast for the entire staff. She made scrambled eggs, bacon, hash browns, and muffins. The staff thoroughly enjoyed her meal and concurred with everyone who ever tasted her food that she was an excellent cook. I realized that when she was released, she would continue to need ongoing therapy and around-the-clock attention at home.

* * * * * * *

At 72, after 50 years of serving the United States, I was more than eligible to retire and did so in January 2012. I suggested we relocate to our lake house and continue her outpatient therapy in Abingdon. She liked the suggestion so she could be close to Tina and her family. She found a new general practitioner and a team of specialists. Her condition seemed to be improving but then, for some unknown reason, (perhaps God was ready for her to come home), her body parts started failing. She lost blood circulation in her legs. We tried everything, even acupuncture. We requested, but the doctors denied, hyperbolic chamber treatment as they thought it would do nothing to help.

When there was nothing more that could be done, Zeets entered home Hospice care. She was in a lot of pain and all I could do was administer morphine to comfort her. Both children and their spouses and all the grandchildren were with us. She was able to say goodbye to everyone. On July 30, 2013, she went to be with God. She was 70 years old. We had been married for nearly 49 years.

I had a Memorial Service in Abingdon at Christ the King Catholic Church and then transported her remains to Alexandria for a Funeral Mass at our long-time parish Good Shepherd Catholic Church. The Knights of Columbus had an Honor Guard for her. After the service, there was a large reception in Creedon Hall sponsored by the women of Good Shepherd and the Mount Vernon Council KCs. About 700 guests attended including relatives, friends, neighbors, parishioners, yacht club members, coworkers, and many of the medical personnel who cared for her over the years. After the service, Zeets was transported back down south. She was laid to rest in a crypt at the Catholic cemetery at Saint Anne's Church in Bristol, Virginia where I will be laid to rest beside her one day.

2014-2025

SECOND LIFE

CHAPTER 36
THE ARRIVAL OF CINDY

A couple of weeks after Zeets' death, I enrolled in a grief support group sponsored by the funeral home in Abingdon. Although her death was expected and not sudden, it still left me in shock and severe emotional pain. I did not want to resort to medication as some had suggested. I was hoping the group would help me through this time of great stress and maybe it did help a little. However, after a few weekly meetings, I was still suffering very much.

I continued driving the 5 1/2 hours between Abingdon and Alexandria tending to the maintenance of both homes and continuing to work with the KCs in Alexandria. One Sunday about nine months after Zeets' death, I was at the Knights' Pancake Breakfast in Alexandria and had a discussion with two elderly sisters who were widows of former Knights who lost their lives in the Vietnam War. We shared our stories of loss with each other. They both mentioned they had attended group grief counseling at The Haven, a Catholic organization. One sister said it helped her a great deal, but the other did not feel she benefitted much from the experience. They gave me the contact information before I departed that day.

The next day, I called and was told that the next session would begin in two weeks and would meet for two hours every Saturday morning for 12 weeks. I was encouraged to attend so I registered over the phone. I was unsure if it would help my situation, but I was willing to try. A few days later, I received a call and was told they had so many participants that they were going to do an afternoon session as well. They asked which time slot I preferred, and I chose mornings.

There were ten of us in the morning session, seven women and three men led by two moderators, a man and a woman. They were well-trained, professional, and compassionate. Across the room from me there was a very attractive lady named Cindy. When we went around the room to talk about ourselves, she sounded pleasant. She was articulate and very intelligent. She was Catholic and I was not ready to spend the rest of my life alone. I began paying more attention to her.

After about a month, one morning five of us lingered in the lobby after the session and continued sharing the struggles of our new reality. We were talking about how difficult it was to go into a restaurant alone and how we couldn't do so yet. I could tell that Cindy was in deep pain. I put my arm around her shoulder and said, "I think I can help you. I will go out to dinner with you." She accepted but was headed out of town for work, so we made plans for a few weeks away, the Saturday evening of Memorial Day Weekend.

I showed up at her home with a big bouquet of roses I had picked from my Mount Vernon home garden. I made reservations for 5:30 pm at Ruth's Chris in Crystal City. We talked about where we grew up, family, our education and careers. It was truly a congenial evening. About halfway through the evening, the dinner began feeling more like a date. We discovered we both loved martinis. I liked gin on the rocks and she liked dirty vodka straight up. We bonded over our dislike of croutons and kept trying to give them to each other. We were used to giving up our croutons because both of our spouses had loved them. The waiter came by and said he was sorry to interrupt but wanted to know if there was anything else he could do for us. When we looked around, we realized we were the only two people left. The chairs were up on the other tables, and someone was running a vacuum cleaner. It was time to go. I drove her home and at the door thanked her for a delightful evening and asked her permission for a good night kiss. She agreed and we had a friendly kiss. I asked her for another date the following Saturday night and she accepted and we said good night.

* * * * * * *

Occasionally while dating Cindy, I would reflect on my college years when Father MacEvoy encouraged me to consider becoming a Jesuit priest. However, I knew I was much too old. Early on in our relationship, Cindy and I went to the Franciscan Monastery in Washington D.C., and I was impressed particularly with their outreach work in the community as well as their gardening and woodworking. I thought that perhaps a monastic lifestyle was what God— The Uncaused Cause— wanted me to pursue. Accepting that as a challenge, I began looking into what was required to be accepted into the Order. I soon discovered that like the priesthood, I was too old to be considered. My fondness for the Franciscan way of life continues to this date and I donate to their mission each year. In return, the mission in Waterford, Wisconsin, sends me many containers of wildflower honey that I thoroughly enjoy and share with family and friends.

CHAPTER 37
MY HOBBY

Working with wood has always been easy and rewarding for me. When I was a youth, I made toys for my sisters and brothers. As an adult, I designed and fabricated storage buildings, helped build barns and houses, renovated recreation rooms, family rooms, and rathskellers. The deck that surrounded three sides of my Abingdon home needed some new railings and spindles. I was unable to find any spindles to match mine in home improvement stores, so I decided to fabricate the replacements myself. After considerable research, I purchased a lathe, a spindle-duplicating machine attachment, and a beginner's set of wood-turning tools from Grizzly and pressure-treated wood from Home Depot. I was on my way to fabricating replacement spindles. In hindsight, I could have replaced all the railings for a fraction of the cost of the lathe. I guess I just needed a reason to get started in woodturning.

The process of removing chips from a piece of wood to produce a product that was visually pleasing captured my imagination. Since my retirement and Zeets' death, I began turning blocks of wood into objects to fill the hours when I was not traveling to Northern Virginia to see Cindy. My initial products vacillated between rough and disastrous. Most found their way into the wood-burning stove in my workshop. But, at least, I was kept comfortably warm in the cooler months. My source of wood (apart from that purchased for the spindles) was whatever was given to me. Almost all of it was fallen trees or cut by crews clearing utility lines. With my enormous wood mortality rate, there was no way I could justify purchasing exotic or expensive wood as much of it would ultimately end up as heating fuel.

I was intrigued by my newly acquired pastime. Although I was able to produce the necessary number of acceptable spindles, I realized my self-teaching approach would only get me so far. I located a Woodcraft store in Roanoke, a two-hour drive from my home, that offered woodturning classes on Saturdays. I enrolled in two classes where I learned how to sharpen tools, mount pieces of wood into a lathe, hold tools and apply them to the wood for smooth, clean cuts. My first two projects were a bowl and a mallet, both of which I proudly display in my home. With my new knowledge, and the purchase of many additional tools, my wood mortality rate was rapidly dropping.

Soon I became comfortable showing Cindy the results of my efforts. She became my first fan and supporter. I joined the Tri-Cities Woodturners Club in Gray, Tennessee about an hour and half from my home. The club was an enormous source of information about types of wood and techniques for turning, sanding, and finishing craft articles for shows. Several of my fellow woodturners invited me to visit their workshops, and one of them demonstrated turning and finishing a salad bowl for me.

The Tri-Cities Woodturners Club meets the first Tuesday of every month. Before the business meeting we have a social hour and an "Instant Gallery." Members bring their works of art and explain how they made them and what makes them special, as well as addressing questions and comments from other members. The other member's products humbled me but also gave me a glimpse into what I might accomplish in the future. Most of the members are retired and have been turning for many years and a few are very active selling their products.

One of the members is legally blind. He has a store attached to his workshop. He sells his work and gives woodturning lessons. Another artisan told me he purchased an exotic piece of wood for one thousand dollars. When my jaw dropped he said: "Don't worry, I made two bowls from it. One sold for $8000.00 and the other for $7,600.00." I silently concluded that I would stick with free wood and making gifts for friends and relatives. I developed a policy that whenever someone gave me wood, I would give them the first bowl I made from it. I have acquired a large supply of wood including black walnut, English walnut, wild cherry, oak, maple, chestnut, Bradford pear, boxwood, and apple.

The quality and artistic flair of my products had improved exponentially. Cindy and some of my fellow wood turners no longer allow me to call myself a novice. I have been to many craft shows, including juried shows where I had to be selected to attend. I proudly wear my tee shirts that read, "I turn wood into things. What's your superpower?" and "Ask Me About My Bowls." I never tire of watching people run their fingers along my work and exclaim how beautiful they are and how talented I am. This hobby has kept me very active, physically and mentally, in my retirement years. Since God gave me this talent, I am willing and anxious to share my techniques with others.

Tom, the artisan woodturner

CHAPTER 38
THE SECOND APEX

The mountains were smoking one spring morning in 2024. The temperature had been fluctuating between cooler and warmer than usual. There was a slight drizzle and a fair amount of cloud coverage. The sun's rays were finding it difficult to penetrate through. The forest across the lake on the mountainside produced cloud-like patches of white steam. Like most mornings I crawled out of bed at 5:00 am, got the coffee percolator going, poured a steaming hot cup, and sat on my covered back deck swing slowly allowing the day and my life to begin. Retirement is wonderful. There is no urgency at 5:30 am, it is my favorite time of the day. It is also the time I think, just letting my mind wander and it is when I try to say my morning prayers.

That morning, my mind bounced back to my days on the Gemini program and the complexity of its detailed design. Then I started to think about the segmented bowl I was turning for my granddaughter Megan's graduation gift. She requested I make her a bowl so that she could have to remember the milestone and me. I made a freehand drawing of the bowl I wanted to create with six rings of wood glued together. Each ring is comprised of 24 individual pieces. Three of the rings are a combination of Spalted maple and English walnut. The other three rings are oak. Each piece is a trapezoid cut at a 7.5-degree angle on each side. The precise angles are necessary so that when assembling the ring, everything fits together snugly.

Then I started thinking about God— The Uncaused Cause— who is infinite energy. I was about to work with a piece of wood to produce an article. I made a sketch, determined the dimensions, angles, height, and diameter. I then considered the types of wood, their grains and strength, and lastly which finish to use. Equipped with the knowledge of my plan and the necessary materials, I would undertake the task to produce the bowl. Since I am energy, and God is infinite energy, then I am an image of The Uncaused Cause. Because I required knowledge and a plan to produce the bowl, I understand that God also has the knowledge of His plan and the materials to make all from energy. Working with infinite energy, His knowledge must also be infinite. God's knowledge, like His energy, is not created, nor is it destroyed. However, for humans, knowledge only comes incrementally as we develop and mature.

Thinking back to my fourth-grade project of God in three persons in the equilateral triangle of the Trinity, I now felt I could identify the second apex of my triangle— Knowledge. But suddenly my attention was diverted to two purple martins flitting back and forth, alternately bringing food to their offspring nestled in one of the cubicles of my birdhouse. As they approach with the morsels, the little chicks poke their heads out of the opening. I raised my binoculars to see two little yellowish beaks eagerly awaiting their parents' offerings. The process of flying back and forth seems endless and gives new meaning to the term "Door Dash." It was time for me to pull myself away from the spectacular nature show and go to my shop to put my plans into motion.

CHAPTER 39
DATING

After our first "date" to Ruth's Chris, Cindy and I completed our grief counseling group meetings at The Haven. Seven of the ten in the group agreed to continue meeting weekly on our own at Kilroy's, a nearby bar and grill. Despite the 5 1/2 hour ride from my home in Abingdon, I attended most every meeting. I was enjoying Cindy's company and we were going other places together such as my yacht club, KC events, and church. I was also protecting my interest in Cindy from another suitor in our group who was in his early 40s. He soon gave up the chase. Personally, I did not think he ever had a chance!

My trips to the Alexandria area were synchronized to see Cindy as well as maintain my house and boat and to stay active in the Coast Guard Auxiliary and the KCs. After six months of dating, I invited Cindy to my home in Abingdon, in the country on a lake. To get to the house, you get off the I-81 South at exit 19 and then travel 7 ½ miles on twisting, turning two-lane country roads, the last mile, Lakeshore Drive, being a private road. Understanding that Cindy was a die-hard city girl (raised in Detroit and having lived in Metro D.C. for 30 years) I was unsure how she would react to the very rural Deep South. Therefore, I suggested she meet me in the parking lot of Lowe's at exit 19. We left her car there and I did the driving.

We went to lunch at the Wildflower Café and grocery shopping at Food City. Cindy commented that so many people in my town had southern accents. On the drive to my house, she repeatedly exclaimed, "There is nothing out here!" By the evening, I could sense she was homesick for the sounds of police sirens, honking horns, and screeching tires. She adjusted to the natural beauty and solitude by the end of the weekend. However, I did entertain the idea of purchasing a city sound CD for her to listen to at bedtime before her next lake house visit.

* * * * * *

Cindy loves to travel and had done so for work and with her late husband Jeff and daughters Sarah and Rachel. I had done a fair amount of traveling with Zeets until her health prevented us from taking long trips. One day, I received a brochure from Oceania Cruise Line for a trip to the Mayan Riviera. The ship was going to Mexico, Guatemala, Honduras, Belize, the Cayman Islands, and Key West, Florida. What made this cruise very attractive was the prospect of meeting up with my sophomore year Marquette roommate, Leroy Taegar. I often wondered if "Sess" ever made it through medical school, became a doctor, and returned to Belize to practice medicine. I was hoping to surprise my old roommate and get the answers to those questions.

There was no difficulty selling Cindy on the idea of the cruise. She was ready to travel anywhere. She put in the request for leave and we booked the trip. When the ship docked in Belize, we went on a shore excursion to Mayan ruins. I asked everyone we encountered if they knew Leroy Taegar. I kept striking out, no one I asked knew anyone by that name. Finally, I asked our local guide (who was about my age) if she knew him. She replied, "Do you mean Doctor Taegar?" I was so happy to find out he had achieved his goals and told her so. I explained that we had been college roommates 60 years ago. I asked where I could find him. She told me that, sadly, he had passed away two years ago. I asked if he had any children and if I could meet them. She said he had a daughter who owned the very tour company she worked for, but because she was the big boss, it would not be appropriate.

* * * * * * *

After dating for a while, my son Tommy and his wife Danny met Cindy and I for dinner in Tyson's Corner. Soon after they agreed to introduce Cindy to their daughters, Julia and Isa. We went to a lovely Italian place in Georgetown called Filomena. Isa said she expected Cindy to be a "little old lady with gray curls." More time was going to be needed for Tina to be willing to meet the new lady in my life.

CHAPTER 40
PETEY ARRIVES

On August 29, 2015, Cindy and I were riding our bikes on the Creeper Trail. The Creeper is a 34-mile rail to trail traversing two counties from Abingdon to Damascus, Virginia ending just past White Top station in the Mount Rogers National Recreation Area. We had been riding there as often as possible since September 2014 when I gave Cindy a mountain bike for her first birthday that we spent together. During our rides, Cindy would yell out things like "Jogger on your left" or "Rocks on the path." That day she shouted, "Impossibly cute dog ahead." When we stopped at a bench to take a water break, that impossibly cute dog caught up with us and jumped into my lap.

He was being walked by two Emory and Henry College students. One of the ladies, named Kathy, told us they had found "Peanut" in a box in a gas station restroom in December 2014 when they were driving from Virginia to New Jersey for Christmas vacation. Kathy and her roommate shared a small apartment and each already had a large Australian Sheepdog, so they were trying to find a forever home for Peanut.

I kept insisting I was not ready for a pet because I felt it would tie me down. However, Cindy pointed out that I was always very sad and lonely after her visits and a dog might help. Cindy had three cats and said they really helped with the loneliness after Jeff's death. She also pointed out that I often "borrowed" my granddaughter's dog Cleo even when she didn't need a dog-sitter because I liked the company. Cindy took pictures of Peanut and got Kathy's phone number.

That evening, I couldn't stop thinking about Peanut. I grabbed a pad and pencil and wrote down dozens of questions including, "Is he housebroken?" and "Does he travel well in a car?" I called Kathy and began asking my questions. My final question was, "If it doesn't work out, will you take him back?" Kathy was emphatic that if I couldn't keep the dog, I had to give him back and promise not to take him to a shelter. She also wanted to come see where I lived before she would agree to letting me have him. I told her to bring a friend because I lived far out in the country. Cindy had already left because she had to be at work the next day.

A few days later, Kathy, her friend and Peanut showed up. Peanut immediately jumped into my lap. I took them around the house, my shop, and the yard. Kathy agreed that I would be a good dog daddy. She entrusted Peanut to me, along with some food, and his collar, harness, and leash. I told Kathy I would like to change his name. Secretly, I wanted a more manly name for him, but not too different from what he was used to. I settled on Pete. However, very soon it turned into Petey. He has been my beloved and faithful companion since that day. No one could ask for a better dog.

I have over three acres of grass to cut. The first time I had to cut the grass after Petey arrived, I wasn't sure how he would react to the tractor. I put him on the back deck that runs the length of the house and he walked back and forth following my progress. Soon after, he would sit under a big shade tree and watch me when I cut the grass.

The next time Cindy came to visit, I asked her to call when she got off the freeway and was making her way to the house. Petey and I waited in the guest bedroom where the windows look out to the street. I sat in an armchair and Petey stood on his hind legs with his paws on the windowsill. I am sure he didn't know exactly what he was looking for, but he was excited and sensed something special was about to happen. When I spotted Cindy's car, we went outside and he ran to her. Cindy stopped and opened the car door and Petey hopped in her lap for the ride into the driveway. That became their ritual, and he does it to this day.

Petey is a very inquisitive and intelligent dog. He seems to understand whatever Cindy and I talk about. His favorite activities are walking the Creeper Trail and trying to chase rabbits and squirrels. I wonder if he remembers that the Creeper is where we met him. Petey's other favorite things are running errands to Lowe's, the bank, and the pharmacy where everyone pets him and gives him treats. I always keep a pocketful of treats in case Petey meets someone who doesn't have one handy. He also loves attending picnics at our church, going on boat rides to the marina, dancing with Cindy to "Hound Dog" at the winery, and visiting with my granddaughter's dog Cleo.

There used to be a brewery in our town in an old icehouse. We were regulars there and Petey was the unofficial mascot. He would even jump on stage with the bands. About two years after Petey and I became inseparable, we were at the brewery when I noticed a lady who looked familiar. It was Kathy. Our eyes met and she mouthed, "Is that the dog?" I said, "Call him by the name you gave him and let's see what happens." She called "Peanut." Petey's ears perked up and he ran to her and jumped in her lap and smothered her with licks. After a few minutes, he ran back to me and jumped in my lap as if to say, "Don't worry daddy. I'm still your dog." A while later as she departed, Petey ran to her to say goodbye. That was the last time we saw Kathy.

Petey does not like the multitude of geese and deer on our property. Cindy hung a sign on our deck that reads, "Deer tremble at my name. Petey!" We must be sure the windows in the car or truck are rolled up because he once jumped out of the moving car to chase a deer. Thankfully, I was only going about 10 mph at the time. Petey's number one enemy is any dog on television. When he sees a dog in a movie, TV show, or commercial, he jumps off the couch, runs to the TV, and growls and barks. He tries to go behind the TV to chase the intruder out of his house. We can't watch the Westminster Dog Show or the Puppy Bowl without endless howling and barking. Fortunately, he has no objection to actual dogs in the house.

Petey is my constant companion. He accompanies me for hours in my wood shop, loves to ride shotgun in the car and golf cart, and is the second mate on the boat. When I look into his beautiful brown eyes, it is as if I am staring into the eyes of my beloved childhood companion— Trixie.

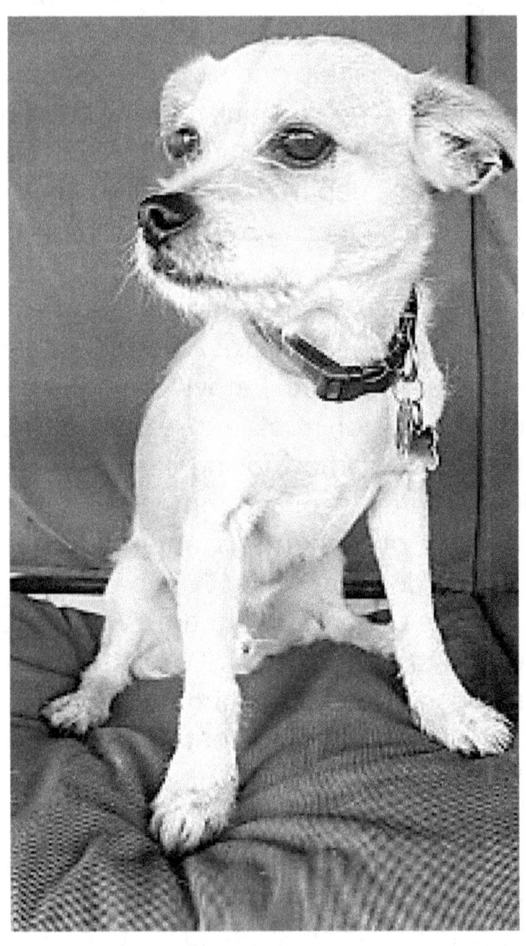

Petey

CHAPTER 41
TRAVELING

I never traveled in my childhood. We only left the farm to go to town for supplies, attend church and school, or to visit friends and relatives. Each September when I returned to school, my classmates would recount their vacations to interesting places throughout the U.S. I really envied them. The first time I went somewhere new was during my senior year of college for job interviews. I went to Saginaw, St. Louis, Cleveland, and Akron. Although I now realize these are not considered bucket list travel destinations, they whet my appetite to see the wider world.

The very first real vacation I took was my road trip with work buddies the summer of 1964. During my years at McDonnell Aircraft, I traveled on business trips to California, Florida, Texas, and New York. Other than that, the only times Zeets, the children, and I traveled was to visit our families. After I began working for the Department of Defense, I traveled a great deal and often was able to take the family along. The only family vacation we took that was not in conjunction with my work was a long weekend in Branson, Missouri.

* * * * * * *

Shortly after we relocated to Virginia I saw an ad in the paper for a package deal vacation that included flights on Eastern Airlines and a three-day Disney cruise followed by three days at Disney World. Zeets was enthusiastic; however, the children were not. Tina objected on the grounds that cruises were for old people. I won them over by explaining that on a Disney cruise to Disney World, the ship would be filled with children. When we boarded, we were each issued a key to our double bunk bed cabin. Our only rules were that the children meet us for meals and return to the cabin at a reasonable hour at night. In hindsight, I should have clarified what reasonable meant to a 12-year-old boy.

All went well the first day. However, that night, Zeets woke me to tell me that Tommy was not in the cabin yet. I dressed and went to search for the "boy kid." He was nowhere to be found. I ran into a deck hand and asked if he had seen a boy. He spoke little or no English, so I mentioned the possibility that my son had gone overboard. Overboard was one of the words he understood. We both continued to search for him. I returned to the cabin to see if he was there. I found that the deck hand had beat me back to the room and returned Tommy to Zeets. He said he was just hanging out and talking with a bunch of kids his age in the bow of the boat. Years later at a party, he was regaling other guests with the story of his first kiss that night.

When we docked at Nassau Bahamas, we took a tender to an uninhabited island for a cookout and to go to the beach. Upon entering the cove of Salt Cay, I exclaimed, "I've been here before." Zeets was sure I had not. It turned out that it was the location where the title sequence of the sitcom *Gilligan's Island* was filmed. Unfortunately, Tommy lost his key while swimming. However, when we returned to the ship, we discovered it had been turned in by another guest who found it in the crystal-clear water. We docked in Port Canaveral and the children really enjoyed Disney World, especially because they kept meeting up with the kids they had met on the cruise.

* * * * * * *

After the children graduated from college, Zeets and I began international travel. Zeets suggested we do something special for our 25th wedding anniversary. She wanted to go to Hawaii. She volunteered to take care of all the details. My only request was that she include a boat ride in our itinerary. The first week was a cruise of five islands followed by three days on Oahu and three days on Maui. Halfway through the cruise, we encountered rough seas. The next morning, many of the guests were still ill. Zeets and I felt fine, we were used to boating. I went to the fitness center and found only one other person there. I got on the treadmill next to him and started a conversation with, "It sure was rough last night." He agreed and told me the waves were over 30 feet with the current in one direction and the wind in the opposite direction. He then mentioned he was the ship's captain.

It was a fantastic vacation. I never tasted such delicious pineapple before. We had a case shipped home. The old farm boy in me tried to grow a pineapple from one of the crowns. After about two years, I was successful. My pineapple was about the size of a ping pong ball and did not taste anything like its "mama."

Over the years, Zeets and I took five European river cruises, most of them sponsored by the Marquette University Alumni Association. They were all on small boats with about two hundred guests and were between two and three weeks long. There were informative lectures almost every night about the people, customs, history, and geography of the areas where we docked. We met many wonderful people on and off the river boats and saw majestic landscapes and architecture. The best cruises were the ones we took at Christmas and Octoberfest.

* * * * * *

The most spectacular trip we ever took was our last one together. It began in South Africa with a visit to Robben Island where Nelson Mandela had been incarcerated. Our tour guide was an inmate with Mandela. He told many stories of their struggles and how the inmates communicated with one another. The prisoners wrote notes and inserted them into tennis balls and lobbed them from one court to the other.

We spent a week on safari at Thornybush, a private nature reserve that borders the Kruger National Park. The reserve is home to hundreds of bird species, giraffes, gazelles, hyenas, and the big five: lions, leopards, rhinos, water buffalo, and elephants. Our tour guide was attentive to Zeets' medical condition. She always got to ride "shotgun" in the Range Rover. However, she didn't have to carry a weapon like the driver and the animal tracker. We enjoyed camping in the wild in our open-air cabin. We had outdoor and indoor showers and Zeets was visited by an inquisitive elephant who poked its trunk in while she was showering outdoors. At night, we dined under the stars with the crew and had to chase the monkeys away to keep them from stealing our food. After touring Victoria Falls, we went back to Johannesburg before heading home.

On the flight from Johannesburg to Dulles, we had to refuel on Goree Island, a little French Island off the coast of Senegal, near Dakar. Shortly after we departed Johannesburg, the temperature in the cabin got so hot that everyone was complaining. Zeets became ill and had to use oxygen. Because this was a Marquette Alumni Association trip, there were plenty of doctors and nurses on board. The lead flight attendant told us that when we landed on Goree Island, we would have to get off. I objected to that suggestion and many of the medical personnel agreed with me and said the problem was the temperature in the aircraft. On Goree Island, the crew changed out and nothing more was mentioned about leaving us behind. The temperature problem was fixed during the stop, and we flew to Dulles without any further incidents.

* * * * * * *

I also traveled for work. Many of the trips were highly classified and I was unable to take the family. In fact, only my supervisor and secretary knew my exact location. If Zeets needed to contact me, she would have to go through them. In 1996, as part of the ICAF program, my class took a trip to China to observe their industrial capabilities. We stayed at the White Swan Hotel in Guangzhou, located a few blocks from the U.S. Embassy. All babies being adopted from China departed from Guangzhou. It was a common occurrence to see new parents and their extended family members with their precious adopted children in the hotel. Frequently, especially in the elevators, a chorus of babies would treat us to harmonized wailing until their demands, usually for a bottle, were met.

One Saturday, I woke early as usual and went in search of a cup of coffee. None of my team members were awake yet, so I decided to take a walk and explore the city on my own. As I walked, I heard an unfamiliar sound off in the distance and went to check it out. Soon I reached a park where a group of about 20 senior citizens were lined up in four rows. They were waving their hands and moving their bodies to the music emanating from the portable boom box on the ground. It looked interesting and I had nowhere to be, so I joined in the back row. Soon after the entire group turned 90 degrees to the right and I followed along. After a minute or two, we all pivoted another 90 degrees to the right and now I was in the front row. I felt everyone staring at me. After two more rotations I was safely in the back row again and made my exit. I didn't know it at the time, but I had just participated in my first Tai Chi class.

Moving along through the streets, everyone I encountered greeted me with a friendly nod. I was a foreigner in their land, and they made me feel welcome. Several people tried to engage me in conversation. I am sure that they assumed since I was walking alone I could speak their language. I could not speak a word and relied on the team's translator to communicate. One woman motioned for me to wait and went into her house. She emerged with a young boy about five years old. She spoke to him in Cantonese and then he looked at me and said, "Good morning." I became the language laboratory for him to practice his English. This trip was a life-enriching experience. My travels made me acutely aware that all people come from the same infinite source of energy, God— The Uncaused Cause.

* * * * * * *

Periodically during 2011 and 2012, I traveled to Kyrgyzstan. The Army had an embarkation point there where troops would rotate in and out of Afghanistan during Operation Enduring Freedom. I went there to check on my team, which was responsible for the body armor of troops coming out of the combat zone. They would receive the body armor, radiographically inspect it for damage and place fully functional items back into the supply system for reissue.

On my first trip to Kyrgyzstan, my administrative assistant made the logistical arrangements for me including a hotel reservation at a five-star hotel in Bishkek. I arrived at the hotel very early in the morning. The bellman escorted me to a beautifully appointed, spacious room with two king sized beds. Having traveled for almost 40 hours, I was exhausted and needed a shower. I placed my suitcase on the bed and heard a thump. Checking both beds revealed that neither had a mattress, but rather only a box spring.

After my shower, I put all the bedding from one bed on top of the other to make it as comfortable as possible and caught a quick nap before heading to the facility to meet with my team of contractors. I told them about the unusual situation with the beds in my room and they nodded knowingly and explained that in a Kyrgyzstani hotel, you had to provide your own mattress. I thought they were joking with me, but they told me that they were advised to bring their own mattresses with them from the U.S. They usually ended up selling them to new personnel rotating in who had not been given this tidbit of useful information. If that was the case for a luxury hotel, I shuddered to think of what their motels must be like. On all subsequent trips, the security requirements were stricter, and I was not allowed to stay in town. I had to bunk on the post in the Bachelor Officer Quarters. Thankfully, those beds had mattresses.

CHAPTER 42
TRAVELING WITH CINDY

Shortly after Petey and I became inseparable, Cindy and I started making plans to take more cruises. Therefore, it was necessary to find someone to care for Petey while I was away. My daughter Tina, who lives less than a mile from me, was willing to have Petey stay with her. Petey was already in love with their little white terrier mix, Cleo, so it was the perfect arrangement.

In November 2015, we traveled to Ecuador and cruised the Galapagos Islands. We flew from Quito to Baltra Island and landed on the old WWII air strip that has been repurposed for tourism. After getting our luggage off the plane ourselves, we boarded an old school bus for a bumpy ride to boat, the *MV Legend*. It was clear this was not going to be a luxury cruise! There were 78 passengers and 60 crew. Among the passengers were Jack Hannah and his wife along with his film crew. They were filming a documentary about the islands.

Every morning, we would awake before dawn to go observe the animals on one of the islands. We boarded inflatable Zodiac boats, but they did not deliver us to land, but rather we had to make a 'wet' landing. That meant we were taken close to the shore and had to get out into knee to waist deep water (depending on one's height) and walk ashore so as not to disturb the delicate ecosystem. We were instructed to follow exactly in our guides footsteps and not to take, or leave, anything at all. We were able to witness the animals in their natural unspoiled habitat exactly as Darwin saw them.

On Santa Cruz Island, there was a large tortoise shell at the visitors' center. With her characteristic girlish enthusiasm, Cindy decided to crawl under it for a photo op. After I snapped some pictures, our tour guide announced the departure of our bus. We had a small problem. Cindy easily got into the shell, but there was no getting out. It was too heavy for me to lift alone. We shouted for help and a strong young local man helped free Cindy from her shell and we ran to catch our bus. Each evening, we reboarded the *Legend* hungry and exhausted. There was no entertainment like on typical cruises, but we didn't care. We knew we had to be up before the roosters to do it all again.

* * * * * *

Our next cruise was posh, aboard Oceania *Insignia*, for a trip from Seattle through Alaska's Inside Passage. When we disembarked in Juneau, we visited the Red Dog Saloon to enjoy some drinks and some bawdy piano player entertainment. Afterwards, we went to a souvenir shop because Cindy wanted to pick up gifts for the Marines in her office. I told her I had to use the restroom which was across the street in the town center. She said she would wait for me in the store. I had other plans.

After about 45 minutes, Cindy became concerned and went looking for me. She went to the public restroom and gave a young boy five dollars to go in and look under all the stalls to see if he could find an older gentleman named Tom. The boy said he called out my name, and looked everywhere, but could not find anyone matching that description or name. Cindy retraced her steps back to the Red Dog and souvenir shop, but still no sign of me.

I had a flip phone that I considered as emergency use only, so she called the number. Unfortunately, the phone was in the bedside table on the ship. Cindy called the ship and asked if I had returned. The crew checked their records and told her I was not aboard.

Panic set in and Cindy called the police. A very young officer came and took her statement and a description of me. They got in the police cruiser and drove up and down the streets of Juneau looking for me. Every time the young officer saw an older man, even one in his nineties using a walker he would ask, "Is that him?" Cindy called the ship every 30 minutes to check if I had come aboard. Finally, after hours of searching, the police officer took her back to the ship.

I remember the afternoon differently. When we first got into town, we stopped in a jewelry store. There were several diamond brokers in town. I thought maybe the time to propose was close at hand and this might be a good location to find an engagement ring, but I needed to find out her preference in diamond cut. Later, I used the need to use the restroom as a pretext to go on my secret mission. I could swear I told Cindy I was going to look around on my own and meet up with her later, but apparently, only I thought that.

I spent several hours browsing and talking to merchants in three different stores before purchasing what I considered to be the perfect ring for my wife-to-be. Upon returning to the ship with my precious cargo, I was detained by the officer on duty at the gangway after showing my boarding pass. He began communicating by radio to someone aboard the ship. I was then allowed to board and upon entering our cabin, I was greeted by a relieved, but albeit thoroughly agitated Cindy. She was happy that I was alive and unharmed, but pissed that she, the Juneau police, and ship security had been searching for me for hours. Plus, she even paid a boy five dollars to search a public restroom. After much explaining over a few cocktails, I gave her a souvenir I got for her, a Tanzanite necklace; things calmed down a bit, but not enough. I finally had to confess I had been on a secret mission and that I had bought a ring and placed it in our room safe. I made her promise not to look. She never did.

Upon returning home, I unwrapped the ring and began to feel dissatisfied about the purchase. It was a pear-shaped solitaire, but it no longer seemed big enough. Over the next few weeks, I visited several jewelry stores in Northern Virginia in hopes to trade it in on a larger stone with no success. All of them wanted to sell me a ring but were unwilling to take my ring in trade despite my having documentation for it. I also visited the two jewelers in Abingdon. At last, at Goodman's, I was able to trade it for a beautiful cushion-cut solitaire, encircled by 100 diamonds that was over 3 carats. Now I was waiting for the perfect time to pop the question.

* * * * * * *

During the Alaskan cruise, I mentioned to Cindy that Zeets and I had on more than one occasion tried to entice our children and grandchildren to take a vacation all together (funded by us). We were never able to get an agreement on dates or location. There were a few staunch anti-cruisers and the scheduling proved too difficult. I told Cindy it was a dream of mine to make the family vacation happen. Cindy, a proven master at detailed trip planning, took on the challenge.

* * * * * *

Before the end of the Alaskan cruise, she presented several options for consideration. I suggested she choose one because every trip we had taken turned out great. Cindy laid out the details of a five-day trip in July 2017 to an all-inclusive family-friendly resort in Mexico, Dreams Playa del Carmen on the Mayan Riviera. I agreed to pay for Tina and Tommy and their families, but Cindy insisted on paying her own way because we were still just dating. The trip included flights, hotel, all meals, beverages, and daily excursions.

I decided the trip would be my Christmas gift to my daughter and son, their spouses, and the grandchildren. We planned a Christmas party at the lake house in December 2016 and everyone was there. Cindy made more red, green, and white foods than I ever thought existed. I presented everyone with a booklet that Cindy made with the details of the trip. Tina and Earl and Tommy and Danny had deluxe rooms. Carter, Julia, Megan, and Isa would share a suite. Cindy and I had the Penthouse Suite with a hot tub on the balcony. Cindy's plan was so complete and detailed that there was no dissent. The adults just had to ensure they took the time off work; all the kids would be on summer break from school.

Christmas 2016

We all met up at the Cancun airport. While we were waiting for the shuttle bus to the resort, I made my only request for the trip. Every night at 6 pm, I wanted everyone to have dinner together. There were four restaurants on the property and Cindy had already made reservations at each. From the first dinner on we ended up doing everything all together. We rented ATVs and I insisted Cindy take a turn driving even though she didn't want to. Five seconds into her being in the driver's seat, she ran into the tour guide! He was uninjured and the family continues to tease her about it to this day. We swam in an underwater cave that was filled with bats. Earl and I kept telling terrified Tina and Cindy they were just big butterflies. We hung out at the beach and took catamaran rides. We sunned and swam at the pool (with a swim-up bar). There was a huge 4th of July party with red, white, and blue cocktails and cake, pony rides, an Elvis impersonator, dancing, and fireworks. I think the older children might have gotten tipsy for the first time as they were of legal drinking age in Mexico.

On the last afternoon, Cindy and I finally had a few hours to ourselves before we were to meet up for dinner. We decided to get in the hot tub. I went to take a shower and when I came out, Cindy informed me that the three granddaughters had joined us and were splashing away already. We never got that alone time, but I wouldn't change a thing about that trip. It was a dream come true. It felt like Cindy was now truly part of the family. A few months later, in September 2017, I proposed during the sign of peace at Mass— and she accepted. We went to brunch and I called my grandson Carter and asked him to be my best man.

* * * * * * *

On Christmas 2017, Cindy and I were exchanging gifts. She gave me a glass tree ornament. It was silver with a black silhouette of the Vatican and read, "Rome." I thought it was an odd gift, because we already had enough ornaments to trim ten trees as Zeets and Jeff passionately loved Christmas decorations. I guess I looked disappointed because Cindy said, "Don't you love it? Aren't you excited?" She started giggling and pulled out a large envelope filled with airline tickets, hotel reservations, and concierge tickets to the Vatican, Sistine Chapel, and Coliseum. She also had reservations for a New Year's Eve bash in Saint Peter's Square. She said we would depart on December 28th for a week in Rome. I was concerned that Petey would have to go to a kennel, but Cindy already arranged it with Tina to keep him. She had also secretly packed our bags. Cindy had been to Rome a few times before and worked with a travel agent to craft a perfect itinerary.

On Saturday evening, we attended the Vigil Mass at Saint Patrick's, an English-speaking church. After Mass, we were greeted by the pastor who recognized us as visitors. We asked where he would recommend we go to dinner. He suggested a restaurant owned and operated by one of his parishioners called Da Giovanni. He said it was just a few blocks away from the church. It turned out that Italian blocks are considerably longer than American ones, because we walked for over a half mile down cobblestone streets and alleys. It seemed like we were in a sketchy part of town. We finally arrived and had to go down a steep, dark stairway to the entrance.

When we opened the door, we were a little apprehensive until we told the man who greeted us that Father from Saint Patrick's sent us. You would have thought we were the owner's long-lost relatives! The cocktails were strong and the food was delicious. All the other patrons were locals and greeted us warmly. We only ordered two entrees, but many specialty items of appetizers, soups, and desserts arrived on the house. It was delightful and by far our best meal in Italy.

Everything about the Vatican was awesome. I had a very moving experience when I viewed the Pieta in Saint Peter's Basilica. I thought of Michelangelo going to the quarry to choose a block of marble for his masterpiece like me going to my woodpile and selecting a block of wood to create one of my "masterpieces." On New Year's Eve, we took a taxi to the restaurant in Saint Peter's Square. It was a twelve-hour party. There was a dinner followed by dancing. After ringing in 2018 with a champagne toast and black-eyed peas, the party continued till morning and concluded with a sumptuous breakfast buffet. We had to sleep through most of New Year's Day.

Dancing to "The Twist"

CHAPTER 43
A YEAR NOT TO BE FORGOTTEN

For the five years since Cindy and I met in grief counseling at The Haven, we were constant companions. She lived in her home in Alexandria, and I split my time between my Mount Vernon home and my lake house in Abingdon. Also, I occasionally stayed aboard *Tom's Toy II* at the Mount Vernon Yacht Club. My two houses were hours apart, but I was retired, and the distance didn't cause any hardship. Cindy was still working, but eligible to retire. She was able to make the trip down to Abingdon once a month.

During those five years, I sold my Mount Vernon home and the boat and began to live at the lake house full time. Those years gave my children and grandchildren the opportunity to adjust to Cindy being my faithful and loyal companion. The same was true for Cindy's girls. Both Cindy and I felt that God had brought us together and had a definite plan for us, but He had yet to reveal it.

* * * * * *

In January 2019, Cindy and I took a cruise to Cuba. The travel ban had been lifted at the time and U.S. citizens were allowed in for tourism. Cindy was interested in visiting the Hemingway house and haunts as she has a master's degree in literature. I was interested in the island nation that almost brought the United States and the world into a nuclear war in 1962 with the Cuban Missile Crisis. We wanted to see what life was like under Castro's regime firsthand. The Salon Parisien Cabaret was beautiful. There was music, dancing, singing, and fabulous costumes. Even though I do not understand the Spanish language, it was stunning. If that was all I saw, I would have a wonderful image of life in Cuba. However, there was more to see.

The people do not own anything, even their homes. The government tells the Cuban people where to live and when to move. Every structure showed signs of wear and neglect. Vintage cars from before Castro took power in 1959 were kept in mint condition. The bodies and paint jobs were pristine. However, those 1950s Chevys did not sound like anything I ever heard before. I could only guess what was under the hoods. One of our tour guides, a mechanical engineer, was allowed to quit her job and pursue a career in tourism. She was making more money (mostly in cash tips she probably didn't report) and could finally afford a cell phone for the first time in her life.

Another tour guide had a PhD in Economics. He told us he had been invited to present a paper at a university in California. The Cuban government authorized him to make the trip; however, his wife and children had to stay behind to prevent him from defecting. He forgot to pack a razor and asked his driver to stop at a store so that he could pick one up and shave before his speech. The driver stopped at a 7-11. He recounted how he fell to his knees and cried when he saw row after row of things to buy. He had heard stories about American plenty, but he was never sure if they were true.

The adults in Cuba seemed to be just existing, most had frowns on their faces and looked unhappy. Not so with the children. They were all dressed in their school uniforms and seemed to be filled with joy, chatting and playing with friends. I told Cindy that I wished more Americans could experience Cuba because it would change the liberals' minds with their lofty ideas of socialism and communism.

* * * * * *

In February 2019, Cindy, Petey, and I drove to Florida to visit Tommy and his family in their new home. We stopped overnight in Savannah, Georgia. We spent several days with them and had a wonderful time. Petey especially enjoyed himself. He caught his first gecko by the tail and was stunned when the tail of his prize snapped off in his mouth and the gecko kept running. On the ride down, I pinched a nerve in my back and that put a damper on things as I couldn't do much physically. On the trip back, we stopped overnight in Charleston, South Carolina. We went to the Black Fedora Comedy Mystery Theater. Cindy volunteered to act a part in the audience participation play and stole the show in Sherlock Holmes "Other Brother by a Southern Mother." She also won a prize for identifying the most television and movie detectives.

The pain in my back was excruciating on the trip from South Carolina to Abingdon. Cindy had to drive the entire way through horrible thunderstorms. Upon returning home, we went to the ER and I had an MRI. Spinal surgery was scheduled and performed in March just before my 79th birthday. Instant relief! What a blessing.

* * * * * *

On June 29, 2019, the big day finally arrived. Over the previous five years, Cindy and I spent a lot of time together and did many different things. We had been attending Mass and taking Communion weekly. Over those years, we worked from adjusting our lives without Zeets and Jeff to a new normal. We also worked out a financial agreement. We had many discussions about the wedding, particularly about who to invite. Cindy wanted a large wedding, but when we added up the friends and relatives on both sides, it seemed impossible to decide who to invite without causing hurt feelings. The simple and safe solution was to limit it to our children and their families.

We were married at Christ the King Catholic Church by Father Francis, our Pastor. My brothers Knights of Columbus provided an Honor Guard. My grandson Carter and granddaughter Isa were the witnesses. Rachel carried the Cross, Tommy and Sarah did the readings, and Tina, Megan, and Julia brought up the gifts. My son-in-law Earl acted as photographer. Three times before the end of the vows, Father Francis had to tell me it wasn't time to kiss the bride yet. I thought the ceremony was long, but I couldn't hear him very well because I still had my old hearing aids. After the ceremony, we had a reception dinner and dancing at one of our favorite restaurants, *The Tavern*.

* * * * * * *

Tom and Cindy's wedding

The night before the wedding, we had a rehearsal at the church and a dinner at our house. During the celebration, Tommy announced that through his '23andMe' DNA testing, he had been able to locate his birth parents. To this day, he never explained what motivated him to pursue finding them. Of course, he knew he was adopted. Zeets and I talked openly to both Tommy and Tina about their adoptions. From the time he was only a few weeks old, I was his dad. I believe Danny encouraged him to find his birth parents to drive him further away from me. Ever since she came into our lives, she actively interfered with our relationship with Tommy. She wanted complete control over Tommy and did not want us to influence him in any way.

I had changed his diapers. I prayed for him during his eye surgery and wished I could do it in his place. I was there for all his sports: football, soccer, baseball, and basketball. I cheered him on and coached him. I was his assistant scout master and helped and encouraged him to achieve his Eagle Scout and Order of the Arrow. I assisted him through his academics and early job challenges. Zeets and I were real parents to him— his only parents. I felt pushed aside and rejected; it was as if he was in search of someone better. I truly felt that if Zeets were alive, this would have broken her heart. She loved Tina and Tommy with everything she had. She called Tommy her "Boy-Kid."

I was so hurt, I had to leave the party. Cindy found me in the master bathroom crying my eyes out and tried to comfort me. I certainly hope Tommy never experiences the pain this caused and continues to cause me. Since that time, he and I have had a few minor discussions on the subject. It seems to me that he has said all that he wants to say. Maybe I am hurt because I have always been a very protective dad. I tried to never let anything hurt my children or take them from me. Maybe I am also jealous and possessive, and I don't want to lose Tommy Joe, our "Boy-Kid." My pain persists and I feel certain he doesn't comprehend what he has done to me.

* * * * * * *

On July 3, 2019, after all the wedding guests had departed, Cindy's sister Elenor, brother-in-law Tony, and nephew Jake arrived. They made the road trip from Detroit to spend a week vacation with us. On the Fourth of July, we spent the day swimming and fishing from the dock and sharing family stories. It took effort to keep Petey from eating Jake's fish bait, which was leftover fajita meat because he didn't want to touch a worm. Ultimately we failed and Petey ate it all. We had just finished a bar-b-que dinner and were waiting for Tina and her family to arrive for the fireworks. As I was getting ready to take a shower, I experienced a tremendous pain in the center of my chest.

The pain was so severe I fell on to the bed. I laid there for a moment, but the pain persisted. I assumed I was having a heart attack, so I took two aspirin. I got back in bed and waited for the pain to go away, but no such luck. A short time later, Cindy came in and before she could say anything, I told her to call 911. The ambulance arrived very quickly. The EMTs checked my vital signs, gave me nitroglycerin and loaded me into the ambulance with Cindy in the front seat next to the driver. Cindy called Tina and Earl to tell them what was happening, and they drove straight to the hospital and met us there.

At the hospital, they conducted tests and determined that I had not had a heart attack. I had a splitting headache from the nitroglycerin, so they inserted an IV to administer fluids. I kept asking for something for the pain, but the nurse said my blood pressure was too low; it had dropped to 60/30. Hours later, they continued to give me fluids and told me they were going to keep me overnight for observation and Tina and Earl went home. When my blood pressure did not improve, the ER doctor suspected I might have blood clots in my lungs, so he ordered a CT scan with contrast. Luckily, I had surgery at that hospital a few years before and there was a CT scan on file. The ER doctor compared them and phoned the on-call surgeon at the Heart Institute in Johnson City, Tennessee, and then ordered another series of CT scans. After the CT scans, I was lying on the exam table with Cindy next to me. She heard the doctor on the phone ordering a MedEvac helicopter to take a patient to the hospital in Johnson City for emergency surgery. She told me and we prayed for that poor person. We didn't realize at the time that it was me. Unfortunately, the weather was too bad, and I had to go by ambulance. The EMTs took Cindy home and she got in our car and started toward Johnson City.

It was a long bumpy drive. The EMTs were silent, which was alright with me because I was not in the mood for conversation. When I was wheeled into the operating room, I was greeted by bright lights and no less than 18 personnel in white gowns with face masks and shields. They immediately began inserting IV needles and one started shaving my legs. I felt like telling that person that wasn't where I was having pain. A tall, rotund man with a booming voice told me he was my doctor. There wasn't much time for conversation because several attendants were sliding me onto the operating table, but I managed to get in a few sentences in. I asked, "Are you a good doctor?" He replied, "I think so." Then I asked, "What are my chances?" Later I would find out the answer to this question was designed to get my assistance and put me in a positive state of mind. The doctor said, "If we do nothing, you will not make it through the night. With the surgery, you have a 75% percent chance of surviving." With that news I said, "Let's rock and roll." I was out like a light for the eight-hour surgery and didn't wake up until two days later.

When I awoke, I could feel what seemed like wires holding my chest together. I was in no pain and everything seemed like it was going to be okay. While I was in surgery, Cindy sat all night alone in the waiting room. Tina joined her early the next morning. My surgeon came out to talk to them. He told them the truth— that I only had a 10% chance of making it through the operation. Furthermore, I only had a 10% chance of living for another few weeks. I had suffered an aortic aneurysm. My surgeon told me that the inner lining of my upper aorta had deteriorated and restricted the blood flow causing extreme pain in my chest. He reinforced a section from the valve in my heart and replaced eight inches of my aorta with synthetic tubing. Now I would need to take blood pressure medication, a statin, and aspirin daily and have a CT scan and appointment with him annually.

A few days later, I was moved out of ICU. After two weeks, I was discharged to a rehabilitation center in Johnson City. The care was substandard, and I was having a difficult time recovering. Cindy had to drive back up to D.C. to check in with her job. She called early one morning and heard a lot of commotion in the background. I told her I woke up with severe pain throughout my entire body. She asked to talk to the doctor. A nurse came on the phone and told her they thought I was having a heart attack and they were going to administer nitroglycerin. Cindy, using rather colorful language, told them they were wrong. It was not a heart attack and demanded they put me in an ambulance immediately.

I was taken back to the hospital and admitted. I would not find out for a few more days that I had an allergic reaction to the heparin administered during the surgery. It caused massive amounts of blood clots throughout my body. I needed several blood and platelet transfusions and was under the care of a hematology oncologist for the next few weeks. Unfortunately, I wasn't put in the Cardiac Care unit, but on a general ward. The nurses did not seem to understand all the protocols to care for me. I had to wear a posthorax vest (a heart-hugger) and they were afraid to move me or even get me into the shower. One night, a heavyset nurse came in to check my vitals. Instead of walking around the bed to turn off a beeping machine, she leaned across me and lost her balance and fell on my chest. I was in excruciating pain and screamed loudly. The next morning when Cindy found out, she insisted I be moved back to the Cardiac Care Unit.

Nearly every day, Cindy drove the hour and a half each way to comfort and assist me. She was my advocate with the hospital staff, ensuring all my needs were met. She told me that my little dog Petey had been suffering in my absence. He was not used to me being gone. Every time she came home from visiting me, he would greet her and search for me. She said he whimpered a lot and was throwing up his food. We decided he had to see me before he made himself so sick he would not be able to recover. Cindy snuck him into the hospital. We had a joyful tear-filled (on my part), tail-wagging (on Petey's part) reunion. A nurse came in and told Cindy to hide Petey in the bathroom because the doctor was coming on his rounds.

Cindy began bringing him every time. The staff loved him. He walked by my side up and the down the hallway and stayed with me during my physical therapy. Soon he began visiting other patients as well. One man asked if he could have Petey jump up on the bed to pet him. He said he missed his own dog so much. Petey obliged and played with the man every day. One afternoon, Cindy took Petey to see him, but Petey stopped in his tracks instead of hopping into the bed. The man was gone and a different patient was there. The nurse explained that he had been discharged. Cindy told the new patient about Petey's visits and he welcomed Petey to continue the routine with him. He became the mascot of the ward. Cindy told me that every day on the ride to the hospital she would play a Johnny Cash CD and Petey would stand on the center console and bob his head to the music. If she turned it off or played other music, he would just lay down and mope. As soon as Cindy would exit Highway 26 and turn on to State of Franklin Street, Petey would pant and pace; he knew he was getting close to his Daddy.

On August 1, 2019, I was discharged to a different rehabilitation center in Bristol, Virginia. On August 10, 2019, over five weeks after my aneurysm, I finally came home. Throughout the entire ordeal, my daughter Tina visited almost daily. I enjoyed the time we spent together and the goodies she would bring to me. I truly hoped for a visit from my son Tommy, but that never happened. Cindy did an excellent job keeping our friends, relatives, and my brother Knights appraised of my condition and praying for me. For the next month, I had to attend cardiovascular recovery therapy three times a week. During one session, I mentioned I was having balance issues. They referred me to balance control therapy. During my initial assessment, the therapist determined that the crystals in my ear shifted, probably during my long open-heart surgery. I had to go to two appointments a week for over three months to correct the problem.

* * * * * * *

While I was in the hospital, Cindy was working on a surprise for my homecoming. She flew her little sister Elenor down for ten days and the two of them worked around the clock. They painted the master bedroom and bath and the guest bedroom and bath. Elenor taught Cindy how to make perfect cut lines, refinish the vanity, and install a new faucet. When I came home, I was greeted by a master suite that was transformed into my "Captain's Quarters" complete with a "Poop Deck" (aka bathroom). It was painted four different shades of blue (my favorite color) and decorated with nautical artifacts from my boating days. Cindy also got all new furnishings hand-crafted by an Amish woodworker. It was beautiful. The other rooms were lovely too.

At night, Cindy and Elenor would get carry-out food and watch silly movies. They had a strained relationship for a few years due to the meddling of another sibling. When the Fourth of July visit was abruptly ended, Cindy feared they would not get the opportunity to work on their issues. If there was one silver lining to what I had to go through, it is that Cindy and her sister are now very close. They talk or text daily and have taken several Girls' Trips over the years. As a bonus, I have grown close to my brother-in-law Tony.

* * * * * * *

About a month after I came home was Cindy's birthday. Since we never got to take our honeymoon trip, we decided to go away for a long weekend. Our original honeymoon plan was a pilgrimage to all the Marian

Shrines in France, Spain, and Portugal. However, my doctors advised against air travel or strenuous and extended trips, so our make-up honeymoon was at Jimmy Buffet's Margaritaville Island Resort in Pigeon Forge, Tennessee. We had a wonderful time. We walked around the shops and streets, went to a moonshine tasting, ate dinners in nice restaurants, and watched football games on the big screen TV while floating in the rooftop pool and hot tub. We sported our Bride and Groom shirts with pride. Even though it wasn't the grand excursion we planned, we could not have been happier. I felt lucky to be alive. On the road home Sunday, we found a Catholic Church for Mass and a funky diner for breakfast. The only thing that would have made it better was if Petey could have made the trip, but soon enough he would join us for future Pigeon Forge trips.

* * * * * *

Through my long, slow recovery that fall, I had the pleasure of attending all my grandson Carter's football games at Emory and Henry College and my granddaughter Megan's volleyball games at Abingdon High School. They had the largest and loudest cheering sections of any athletes in town. Tina and Earl, Earls's parents Betty and Danny, and Earls's Aunts, Bobby Sue and Mary Lynn, as well as Megan's best friends Tessa, Jyll, and Kyndall would all be there cheering and ringing the bell.

* * * * * *

In December 2019, Cindy and I drove up to Northern Virginia with Petey. We left him with Sarah and David and took a train to New York City. Cindy had been there countless times and was a great tour guide. We stayed at *The Pierre* across the street from Central Park. It was very chic and even had a doorman and elevator operator. We saw a play on Broadway and the Rockettes at Radio City Music Hall. We took the ferry to Ellis Island and the Statue of Liberty. We almost missed the boat because I followed Cindy, but as she has no sense of direction, we were on the wrong side of the subway platform, heading uptown rather than downtown. We had to make a mad dash and got to the other side just in time. I was very interested in Ellis Island as that was the port of entry into American for my grandfather and his brother.

One evening, we had dinner at the Tavern on the Green and noticed a section with the drapes drawn. Being very curious, I tried to get a peek, but was stopped by the manager and told it was a private party for British Royalty. When Cindy and I stepped outside, we were greeted by numerous camera flashes of the paparazzi who thought we might be Kate and William. When we returned to Northern Virginia, I was honored at the Coast Guard Auxiliary Change of Watch luncheon for my 35 years of service and having served as Flotilla Commander twice.

* * * * * * *

A few days later, we got an early Christmas present. Cindy's daughter Rachel was expecting and was due in early January. However, the baby had a different idea. We were blessed with the arrival of a second grandson, Parker, on December 21, 2019. We stayed up north for a few more weeks to celebrate the holidays with all the visiting family.

Wow, what a decade! My wife Zeets became very ill and died. I had two major surgeries, one with barely any chance of survival. I retired, sold my yacht and home in Alexandria, and moved to Abingdon. I met a wonderful lady who had also lost her spouse and we got married a second time. I took on a trusty companion, my dog Petey. I witnessed the birth of a second grandson. I traveled all over the world. I took up a new hobby. I turn wood into things, what is your Superpower?

CHAPTER 44
THE 2020 DECADE

In January and February, a lot of little envelopes began coming in the mail addressed to Cindy. I was curious and asked what they were. She told me they were responses from her girlfriends about their annual Marine Corps Basic School reunion. At first, I thought it seemed like a very big reunion but didn't think much more about it. Also, like the rest of the world, my attention was on the Covid-19 pandemic. The media broadcasted non-stop (most of which was conjecture and opinion.) Emergency laws and regulations were enacted preventing people from assembling. In March, our Governor made it illegal for more than 25 people to gather in a public space. When that happened, Cindy was forced to reveal the true contents of the little envelopes.

Cindy had been planning a surprise party for my 80th birthday. She booked the ballroom at the Martha Washington Inn and hired a caterer, bartenders, and a DJ. Over a hundred friends and relatives were scheduled to descend on Abingdon. She sent "Save the Date" notices in our annual Christmas card. As unlikely as it seems, over the months of planning, nobody accidentally spilled the beans to me. Cindy cried as she showed me all the plans she made. On my birthday, Cindy made me my favorite meal: filet mignon, lobster tail, loaded baked potato, and carrot cake with cream cheese frosting. She put the 8 and 0 candles on the cake and sang to me. We toasted with champagne. Tina, Earl, Megan, and her friend Tessa showed up with gifts and a huge poster and sang to me through the closed door. It was a bittersweet celebration.

Throughout 2020, I continued turning wood into bowls, all of which I gave away as gifts. Because of the pandemic restrictions, the Knights of Columbus were unable to have their annual scholarship fundraiser at Pizza Plus. Therefore, I donated dozens of bowls to let them sell at "friend" prices after Mass to raise the scholarship money.

* * * * * * *

One of our favorite activities is attending plays at the Barter Theater, the state theater of Virginia located in the heart of downtown Abingdon. Each year they put on over a dozen plays on two stages. The pandemic forced the closure of the theaters. However, the shows went on. The Barter built a makeshift stage in front of the big screen at the defunct Moonlite drive-in theater. Plays were performed on the stage and simultaneously projected onto the big screen with the audio through FM radio. We packed picnics and sat in our car with Petey enjoying live theater at one of the few places in the country where it was able to go on. The other thing we really enjoy is the Creeper Trail. During the pandemic, it was a place we could go to be happy while safely maintaining our distance from others. Before the end of 2020, as more information became available, some of the rigid restrictions were lifted. We were able to witness Parker's Baptism and Cindy's cousin Ryan's wedding.

* * * * * * *

Cindy and I only let the pandemic slow us down for a while and by 2021, we were making contrails in the sky on our way to new and interesting places. In March 2021,

Cindy treated me to a birthday beach trip in Sarasota, Florida. Tommy and his family came down to spend a day with us. My sister Mary and her husband Paul treated us to a day at their Siesta Beach condo and a lovely waterfront dinner. During the summer Cindy and I took a bus tour to many of the national parks out west. We flew into Albuquerque, New Mexico, and started our tour with a few days in Sante Fe. For two weeks, we traveled through seven states and saw Mesa Verde, Monument Valley, the Grand Canyon, Zion, Bryce Canyon, Yellowstone, Grand Teton, and Glacier National Parks. Although I have traveled all around the world and seen many majestic sights, I found our country has scenery second to none. God has really blessed the United States of America. In October, we took a cruise to the Bahamas. It was Cindy's first time on a Crystal Cruise. Shortly after the trip, my left shoulder began to bother me to an extent where I knew I needed to see a doctor. I had two previous surgeries on my shoulder, but now it needed to be replaced.

* * * * * * *

In January 2022, I had a reverse shoulder replacement. The surgery went well, but the physical therapy that followed, although necessary for a full recovery, was very unpleasant. One day in April, Cindy and I were riding in the car and a song she loved by Prince came on the radio. She said, "This was my favorite concert ever. What was your favorite concert?" I told her I had never been to a concert. After she recovered from her disbelief, she got on the internet and booked us a weekend in Savannah, Georgia to see Jimmy Buffet. Next she convinced her cousin Arlene and her husband Steve who live in

Michigan to join us. They were going to an Eagles' concert in Cleveland a few days before and then drove down to join us. The weekend and the company were wonderful. The concert was a blast. I surprised Cindy when I danced and sang along with Jimmy.

* * * * * *

We traveled to Milwaukee, Wisconsin, in June to attend my 60th Marquette University reunion. This was the first school reunion I ever attended. We stayed in a hotel that was a converted Pabst Blue Ribbon brewery. I enjoyed walking around my old campus and seeing how much it had expanded, particularly the college of Engineering. We went on a campus tour, to a comedy show, a dinner dance, and Mass. I also enjoyed being teased about the fact that Cindy wasn't born until after I graduated from college. My only disappointment was that I did not meet up with any of my old classmates from my graduating class. I wish I had attended a reunion sooner.

Tommy and his family visited us for the Fourth of July weekend. It was the first time they came to Abingdon since our wedding. I really enjoyed being with both my children and all my grandchildren at the same time. Later in the month, both of Cindy's daughters and their families came to visit, too. Little Parker was thrilled with the boat. At the end of July, we took a cruise from New York City to Bermuda. While most people, including Cindy, come to the island for the pink sand and turquoise water, what I enjoyed the most was visiting Fort Saint Catherine and talking to the museum curator about Bermuda's role in the Revolutionary War. Another happy memory was standing with one foot on each side of the world's smallest drawbridge, 18 inches wide.

In August, Cindy surprised me with tickets to my second concert, Kid Rock, at the Nissan Pavillion in Northern Virginia. The concert was the kick-off to Cindy's 60th birthday celebration. We also had a party with her daughters and their families. Next, we stopped in Charlottesville, Virginia, to visit my granddaughter Megan at UVA. When we got back home, Tina and her family had another party for Cindy.

* * * * * * *

In October, we flew to Barcelona for a two-week bus tour of Gibraltar and Spain. Cindy and I were surprised by Gibraltar. We expected a big rock but were delighted to find a bustling town filled with shops and dining and caves to explore. In Spain, we traveled to Madrid, Toledo, Seville, Granada, and Malaga. I was impressed that through centuries whether it was Christians, Jews, or Muslims who occupied the land, they preserved the architecture and built on previous masterpieces. While visiting Alhambra, I saw a geometrical design on the wall and sketched it in my notepad. When I returned home, I was able to duplicate it in one of my bowls using 193 separate pieces of wood. Another thing that I really enjoyed was the rail system which was efficient and very fast. The speed the train was traveling was displayed at the front of each passenger coach. At one point, it reached 182 miles per hour, but it felt like we were gliding as the countryside flew by. I wondered why this capability isn't implemented in the United States.

* * * * * * *

We rang in the New Year of 2023 in a mountaintop cabin in Pigeon Forge, Tennessee. Cindy's sister Elenor and brother-in-law Tony drove down from Michigan to celebrate with us. There was a small snowfall, less than two inches, but it made travel up the mountainside nearly impossible. After hours of stressful driving, we finally made it. However, there were so many accidents and abandoned cars that Elenor and Tony had to stay in the town and wait for the roads to be cleared to join us the next day. We played pool and card games. We hopped in the hot tub and went to shows in town. It was a happy way to begin 2023.

* * * * * * *

In April we took a Mediterranean cruise to Spain, France, Monaco, and Italy. It was action packed— ten ports in ten days. We visited the Spanish ports of Alicante, Cartegena, Ibiza, and Mallorca. Every one of them was beautiful. The people were lovely and welcoming, and the food was delicious. France was not as good. We took an excursion to St. Remy. During the hour and a half bus ride from Marseille, our tour guide spoke French with the bus driver and ignored us. Once we got to St. Remy, she left us behind after a restroom break! Since we don't speak French and didn't know our way around, we settled in at an outdoor café and drank wine and people watched.

There was a church across the street and Cindy decided to go light a candle for Zeets and Jeff. After she lit the candle, she said a prayer. When she rose to leave, the Wedding March began to play. She tried to leave but the side doors were locked. She went to the main entrance and pushed the door open. It made so much noise everyone turned to look at her. When she got back to the café she announced that she was so embarrassed we could never return to St. Remy. Monte Carlo turned out to be super rich and snobby. Cindy dreamed of gambling at the casino like James Bond, but it was not open to the public that day. They wouldn't even let us into the hotel lobby bars. We spent the day sitting on a bench near a restroom waiting for the bus to take us back to the ship.

Italy was lovely, especially Pisa. I was intrigued from an engineering perspective about the Leaning Tower of Pisa. During construction, it was obvious by the second story that the tower leaned, but they kept building five more stories. For centuries, architects and engineers tried to straighten, or at least slow down, the listing of the tower using ropes, hydraulics, and other mechanical devices. Our tour guide informed us that recently the tower is beginning to right itself. Beginning in the 1990s, the top of the tower was observed to be moving about a half inch each year. Some scientists attribute the movement to global warming causing the water beneath the tower to rise. Now there is concern about tourism. Nobody is going to travel to Italy to see the Straight Tower of Pisa!

*   *   *   *   *   *   *

One day, Cindy and I were talking with my granddaughter Megan about her upcoming trip to London and Paris with her parents. I told her that I had been to Paris a few times for work and London dozens of times. Cindy heard the Paris stories many times but was confused about the London trips as she had never heard any stories about them. I told her I had changed planes at Heathrow Airport, so I had been to London. Just as with the case of the Jimmy Buffet concert, she went to work planning to get me to London for real.

In August, we flew to London for a weeklong vacation. Cindy surprised me with first class tickets. We saw the changing of the Guard, the Tower of London, Stonehenge, and the Salisbury Cathedral. We had high tea in Kensington Garden, took a moonlight dinner cruise on the Thames, and rode the London Eye. However, for me, the highlight of the trip was the tour of Shakespeare's Globe Theater. The reason it was so important was that I wanted to compare the actual structure to the scale model of the theater I made for extra credit for my English Literature class my junior year of high school. My replica was based on the original structure that was demolished in 1644. The Globe Theater we went to tour was reconstructed in 1997. It is an approximation based on available evidence.

The only difference I could discern were the two columns supporting the balcony that my model did not include. I made my model in the pre-internet world, so I poured over available photographs and based the dimension calculations for it off a person standing next to the building. I have fond memories of my mother sewing little velvet stage curtains to complete the effect. The bonus was that while touring the theater, we were able to witness a dress rehearsal of *As You Like It*.

* * * * * * *

For the entire month of January 2024, Cindy and I took a bucket-list trip. On New Year's Day, we flew from D.C. to Sydney, Australia. After a few days there, we boarded the *Crystal Serenity* and cruised to two stops in Tasmania, through the Milford Sound, and three stops each in the South and North Islands of New Zealand. In Tasmania, we visited an animal rescue. I enjoyed feeding baby kangaroos. Cindy had the thrill of a lifetime when she got to hold and cuddle an infant Tasmanian Devil.

I was very impressed with the cleanliness of the land and the friendliness of the people. If I had to live anywhere but the United States, I would seriously consider New Zealand. The only problem would be that Cindy is allergic to their Monterey Pine trees which are everywhere. Each time we got off the ship for an excursion, she had an allergic reaction that caused hives, rashes, and swelling of her face. She made many trips to the ship's doctor for steroid shots and antihistamine pills. Luckily, on the days at sea, she would bounce right back to normal again.

In February, we took a bus trip with a bunch of Nascar fanatics to experience my first ever race, the great American race— the Daytona 500. Then on February 29, we stood on Cindy's daughter Sarah's back deck and witnessed her getting married to her lifelong love, David.

* * * * * * *

On May 1, I was working in the shop when my right eye vision started to blur at the inner edge. Almost immediately, the blurring was on both edges until it narrowed to a very small circle in the center of my eye. It was like looking through a drinking straw. I sat down to rest and relax. Within a few minutes, my vision was restored. That afternoon, Cindy and I had an appointment to pick up our new Ford Maverick truck that we had ordered six months earlier. We were there a few hours waiting for the sales documents. I casually mentioned to Cindy that something weird happened that morning, I had temporarily lost vision in my right eye. Cindy was in a panic and insisted that we leave and go to the ER. I replied, "This is why I don't tell you when things like this happen." She said I had a choice; she would drive me to the ER or she would call an ambulance. I got in our new truck and she drove me to Johnston Memorial Hospital.

Apparently, the medical personnel agreed with Cindy because I was admitted within minutes of my arrival. We spent that night and the entire next day. They ran many tests and took an MRI of my brain. They determined that I had a Transient Ischemic Attack, a TIA or "mini-stroke." The doctors thought it might have been caused by Atrial Fibrillation (A-FIB), so they fitted me with a heart monitor and put me on blood thinners to prevent another episode. That meant three weeks of waiting and worrying, plus not being able to do any woodworking because if I cut myself I could bleed to death. The results of the heart monitor were negative. I chose to stop the blood thinners and hope for the best. So far, so good.

Later the thought struck me that no one at the hospital ever asked me what I was doing in my shop when the vision loss occurred, and I never thought to tell them. I had been removing the trailer ball hitch from the receiver on the vehicle we were going to trade-in for the truck. The nut was rusted in place. I secured the receiver in a large vise. I tried using a large pipe wrench to remove the nut, but it wouldn't budge. Eventually I applied all the force my body could produce and that was when my vision loss began. After resting and waiting a few minutes, I used an acetylene torch to heat up the nut to a glow and easily removed it with the pipe wrench. That exertion is what I believe caused the "mini-stroke."

* * * * * * *

In late May, there were two joyous occasions. Sarah and David had a small family wedding reception and announced that they were expecting a baby. Cindy and I got to spend a weekend with Tina and her family to attend my granddaughter Megan's graduation from UVA.

* * * * * * *

June found us on a road trip through seven states. We spent the first weekend in Lexington, Kentucky. We went to all our favorite restaurants and toured a racetrack and horse farm. The main purpose of the trip was to visit both our families. My sister Mary opened her home in Bristol, Indiana, for a Pojeta Family Reunion. It was wonderful to see nieces, nephews, and cousins I had not seen in years. Over the past five years, Cindy and I had several visits with all my siblings but one, my brother Bob. I had not seen Bob since my mother's funeral in 2006. Bob drove from his cattle ranch in Nebraska to Michigan to pick up yet another Ellis Chalmers tractor for his collection then drove to Indiana.

* * * * * *

During the reunion, I was especially proud to show off what a fine young woman my daughter Tina had become. She flew there and we picked her up at the airport on our way to the reunion. We got to spend the weekend together sharing photos, eating, drinking, dancing the Twist, and going to Mass on Sunday morning.

Next we drove to Michigan and spent a week at an Air BnB in Wyandotte. We celebrated Cindy's nephew Jake's high school graduation. Cindy was happy to spend a lot of time with her sister Elenor and brother-in-law Tony. We went to a Tiger's baseball game and a comedy club. We also spent time with Cindy's twin cousins Ann Marie and Arlene and our dear friends Amy and Richard.

After our road trip, we hosted several sets of houseguests. Sarah and David came down for a Memorial Day ceremony where a tree at the Veterans Memorial Park was dedicated to Jeff. Tommy spent a weekend. So did Elenor and Tony. Rachel, Steven, Willow, and Parker spent a week. Amy, Richard, and their daughter Justine came down for a week, too. We spent lots of time on the boat and at the winery with all of them. We also hosted a First Friday party with all our friends from church.

* * * * * *

In August, we checked off another one of my 'bucket list' trips. We took a Mississippi River Boat cruise from St Louis, Missouri, to St. Paul, Minnesota. Before the cruise, we spent a few days in St. Louis where I had an opportunity to show Cindy where I spent 20 years of my life. It was where I started my career, met my wife Zeets, and started my family. I took her to the Gateway Arch. It brought back happy memories of the years I spent watching its construction. We toured the museum and rode to the top of the Arch and looked at the city below. The day before, the transport system up the north leg malfunctioned. People were stuck in their tiny compartments for hours until their rescue which included having to climb down. Luckily, we went in the south leg and it was a smooth, albeit claustrophobic, journey. Later we took a sightseeing river boat cruise and joined our fellow travelers for dinner.

One of the highlights of the trip was an actor who portrayed Samuel Clemens (aka Mark Twain). He stayed in character the entire journey, giving lectures and telling stories about the river and Twain's life. He also took us on a guided tour of Twain's boyhood town, Hannibal, Missouri. Cindy was particularly interested because she was planning to teach a class on Twain at the College for Older Adults in Abingdon. I also enjoyed the other guest lecturer, a retired river boat captain, who gave daily talks on his exploits and the lock system. Wherever we happened to be on the river each day, he would tell stories about that area and things he experienced, such as pushing an 18-barge tow up and down the river and going through the locks. As an engineer, I was impressed with the 29 lock and dam structures we encountered. We visited Muscatine and Dubuque, Iowa, and Winona and Red Wing, Minnesota. Of all the places we visited, I found Hannibal the most enjoyable.

After our return home, Cindy became concerned about a dark spot she noticed on her right cheek. The dermatologist took a biopsy and while she was on a girls' trip with Elenor, she got the news that it was skin cancer. In October, she had surgery to remove the basal cell carcinoma and the doctor found and removed a small tumor as well. It took 15 stitches, but the prognosis is excellent. From now on she will have to have regular appointments to catch any reoccurrences as early as possible.

* * * * * *

At 3 am on Thanksgiving morning, Cindy's phone and iPad lit up on her nightstand. We assumed it was either an Amber Alert or a scam artist. A few hours later while drinking our coffee, she was reading her emails and text messages and yelled excitedly that we were grandparents again. Mia was born earlier than her anticipated arrival date of December 14, 2024. Sarah had a difficult 'geriatric' pregnancy, and the baby was delivered by emergency C-section. She was tiny, just over five pounds, but healthy and beautiful.

In early December, we drove up to Northern Virginia. We would have gone as soon as Mia was born, but I had to have my annual CT scan and appointment with my heart surgeon to ensure my replacement aorta was still intact, especially since we were planning an arduous trip in the New Year. We spent ten days with Cindy's daughters and their families getting to know the newest addition, celebrating the many December birthdays and having an early Christmas.

Parker, who I frequently accidentally call Carter, turned five years old and had a Spiderman themed birthday party at a noisy kid-filled venue called Jolly Yolly. I challenged him to a race down the large slide. After a long struggle up many stairs and through tunnels designed for little ones, I finally reached the top. Parker had passed me a few times on my way up and already slid down a few times. We met up and were off. Parker outdistanced me to the bottom by quite a bit even though he went down backwards to give me a fighting chance. When I got to the bottom, I was greeted by the applause and cheers of the parents of the other kids.

When we returned home, we spent Christmas Eve at Tina and Earl's house. After Mass on Christmas Day, we went to Earl's parents' home for Christmas day with the entire family. I have always appreciated Betty and Danny's hospitality and was thankful to be included along with Zeets, then when I was alone after her death, and now with Cindy.

CHAPTER 45
THE LAST CONTINENT

During 2024, Cindy and I reached into our bucket list and withdrew our next destination. We decided to spend a few weeks of summer on a cruise to Antarctica. It was the only continent neither of us had ever visited. As usual, Cindy and her travel agent began formulating a detailed itinerary. In January 2025, we set off on the first leg of the journey, an airplane trip lasting over 24 hours from Tennessee to Atlanta to Buenos Aires, Argentina. Cindy had arranged for a four-hour private tour of the highlights of the city. It was supposed to begin at noon, but due to plane delays we were going to be two hours late. Cindy texted the tour company and got them to agree to come later. We barely had time to drop our luggage in the room and we were off. It was a beautiful 90-degree day. One of the stops was the Metropolitan Cathedral of the Most Holy Trinity where Jorge Mario Bergoglio (Pope Francis) had been the Cardinal.

Tom at the Metropolitan Cathedral

We also stopped at the Casa Rosada and Evita's tomb and monument. While strolling through the Plaza de Mayo, we stopped to watch a lovely young couple perform the tango. I was able to engage a few Argentinians in conversation. All of them expressed that they were pleased that Donald Trump had been elected. They were optimistic that it would help their country's economy. Viking had arranged a nice cocktail party at

259

the hotel, and we met many of our fellow passengers. The next morning, we were off to the domestic airport for a 4-hour flight to the southernmost Argentine city Ushuaia, Tierra del Fuego, where we embarked on an expedition ship, the Viking *Octantis*. Ushuaia is nicknamed "The End of the World." It started as a penal colony where the inmates were forced to build their own prison. The prison was operated from 1902 until 1947 and was reputed to have some of the harshest incarceration conditions in the world. I wasn't expecting it to be much. I was pleasantly surprised to find a resort town with stunning landscapes and a population of over eighty thousand.

* * * * * * *

For the next two days, we sailed about 350 miles across the Drake Passage to the South Shetland Islands. We were told to expect one of two possibilities: the Drake Shake or the Drake Lake. We got lucky and had a relatively smooth crossing. Antarctica is larger in area than the United States and Mexico combined. For the next week, we rode in Zodiacs and Special Operations boats viewing the Melchoir Islands, Hidden Bay, the Lemaire Channel, Astrolabe, Orne Harbor, and Danco Island. We trekked around Damoy Point and explored the former research huts that are now museums. We also went on land at Yankee Harbor and walked around with thousands of Gentoo and Chinstrap penguins. It was incredible, and the best part was the multitude of fluffy penguin chicks. We also saw orcas, blue whales, and Weddell and Leopard seals. Because of the extreme low temperature year-round, all precipitation that falls is immediately converted into ice, resulting in an extremely dry atmosphere. Antarctica is actually the largest desert on earth.

Tom trekking on Damoy Point

Whenever we told anyone where we were going they asked, "Why?" and told us we were going to freeze. Ironically, during our trip, it was warmer in Antarctica (between 30-40 degrees) than it was at home in the Appalachian Mountains. That is with one exception, the day Cindy jumped in the freezing ice-filled water to do the Polar Plunge. For her bravery, she was rewarded with a huge glass of Aquavit and a certificate suitable for framing.

Each day, there were documentaries and lectures on a variety of topics including exploration, whaling, international research, animals, and the environment. The *Octantis* supports scientific research including penguin surveys, climate data collection, and environmental genetic sequencing. The crew released weather balloons, collected phytoplankton specimens, took water samples, and mapped the seabed. There were very strict protocols in place to meet international regulations to minimize environmental impact. Antarctica is breathtakingly beautiful. It is so vast and virtually unspoiled. Cindy remarked that if she were a photographer, she would make a book of pictures and entitle it "Black and White and Blue."

After we came aboard from our trek at Yankee Harbor, I got a toothache which developed into an abscess. Luckily, we had plenty of pain relief due to Cindy's huge First Aid kit, but we did not have the right antibiotic. One of the couples we befriended shared their supply of medicine and I was reasonably comfortable for the next five days that it took to get home. I saw my dentist immediately but had to take stronger antibiotics for a few more days before he could extract the tooth. After I had my tooth extracted, I developed a complication called dry socket and almost a week later ended up in the emergency room due to uncontrollable bleeding. Fortunately, the ER physician is a dear friend and took great care of me.

CHAPTER 46
THE SURPRISE

Around February 2025, Cindy started receiving a lot of mail, email, texts, and phone calls just like February 2020. I began to surmise that the "Basic School Reunion" ruse was on again. I didn't say anything, I just observed and gathered information. There was no way I was going to spoil any possible plans she was making to resurrect my cancelled 80th birthday surprise party. I was told we were having a birthday week for Cindy's sister Elenor and me in Abingdon, Virginia, and Pigeon Forge, Tennessee.

On my birthday, March 21, 2025, Cindy and I met Elenor and Tony at The Martha Washington Inn and Spa. A few minutes later, we met up at our regular brunch hangout with Cindy's twin cousins Ann Marie and Arlene, cousin-in-law Steve, and Aunt Colleen. I was told since the twins had March birthdays, too, they were joining in. We spent the day in the pool and hot tub. At dinner in Sister's restaurant, the group increased with the addition of out dear friends, Amy and Richard. We dined and drank toasts, and they sang "Happy Birthday" to me. We all stayed up late visiting and watching March Madness games in our suite.

On Saturday morning, Cindy's behavior became increasingly suspicious. She kept popping in and out of the suite and was evasive when I asked where she had been. I spent the day hanging out with everyone again. Cindy reappeared midday with an elaborate beehive hairdo. We all showered and dressed for dinner. Cindy disappeared again and my brother-in-law Tony stuck to me like glue ensuring I didn't leave the suite. A few minutes before 6 pm, Tony received a phone call and left. Cindy came to get me, and I assumed we were headed to dinner. However, we didn't go in the direction of the restaurant, but rather toward the ballroom. Cindy explained that there were a few extra folks joining us for dinner.

I was confused as to why we would be meeting a few more friends in the huge ballroom. Cindy opened the door and I was greeted by 150 guests. The DJ (a local bartender and the regular entertainment at Abingdon Winery) announced, "Ladies and Gentlemen, Mr. and Mrs. Tom Pojeta." Everyone stood and clapped and sang "Happy Birthday." I am sure I looked dumbfounded. I just stood there and shook my head for a minute. Everyone yelled "Speech" as the DJ handed me the microphone. One of the guests rushed up with a cocktail— my favorite, a Black Russian. Not knowing what to say, I introduced myself as Cindy's husband and got a big laugh. I thanked everyone for coming and Cindy for all the time and effort she must have put into such a spectacular event. I recounted how she had been working on it for over five years. I spoke a little bit about my life, especially about my love for "The Buddies" – my grandchildren Carter, Julia, Megan, and Isa.

At the end of my speech, I asked Cindy if it was okay if I told a joke suggesting that I could clean it up a little. She shook her head no, but it seemed I was going to tell one anyway. She ran up to me and said that if I told the joke we would have to move. Later, I learned she thought I was going to tell a bawdy joke which she ended up telling it to those who asked, but not my sisters or our priest. I had about a half hour to mingle and greet guests before we had a delicious buffet dinner while the DJ played all the songs that were played at our wedding. The tables were decorated with chocolates wrapped in pictures of me. Cindy made name tags so that all our friends and family could easily get acquainted.

After dinner, the DJ called Cindy and I to the dance floor. We danced to "In My Life" by The Beatles and Cindy cried. Immediately after, the DJ called for everyone to join in for my favorite dance – "The Twist" by Chubby Checkers. Several ladies changed into tennis shoes or flats. I was amazed by the excitement. Everyone danced all night long like we were at a 50's sock hop. Finally, at 11 pm, the DJ announced last call. After hugging everyone good night, we fell into bed for a well-deserved rest.

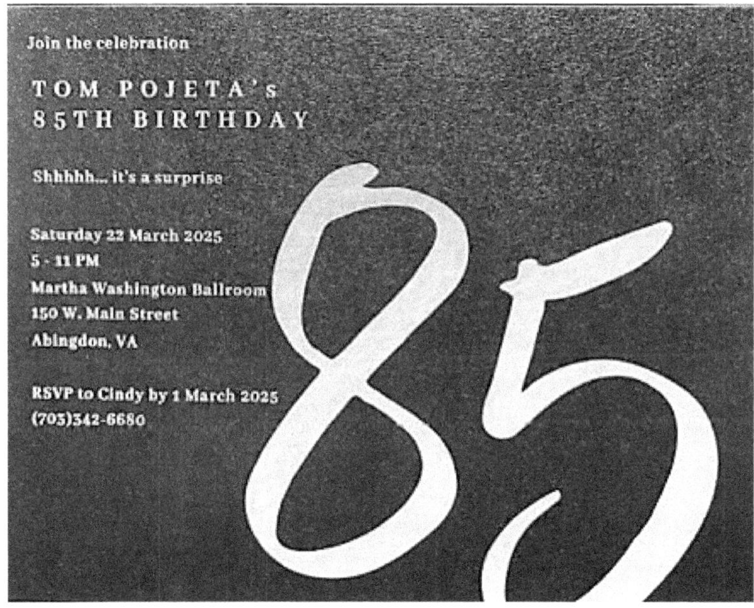

Surprise party invitation

Tom and Cindy dancing to "The Twist"

The next morning, we had to get up very early to attend Mass with family and friends. Cindy invited all the out-of-town guests to our home for a farewell party before they had to get on the road or fly home. I opened my dozens of cards and gifts. On Monday, it was Elenor's birthday and Cindy, Petey, and I met up with her and Tony in Pigeon Forge, Tennessee. We stayed in a beautiful cabin in the woods. We celebrated Elenor's birthday at a rowdy restaurant where the staff insults the guests for fun. Elenor and I stood on chairs and drank a pint of Mad Dog 20/20 to the cheers of the crowd. The next day we went to a Lumberjack contest and, unsurprisingly, Cindy won a prize for being the most enthusiastic audience member. On Wednesday morning, Cindy and Elenor had a tearful goodbye and we drove home. It was a birthday celebration I will never forget.

CHAPTER 47
THE COMPLETE TRIANGLE

On another typical morning at about 5 am, I was on the porch with my cup of coffee. I started saying my morning prayers as I have done countless mornings in the past. However, this morning things seemed to be different. My thoughts are diverted to God— the Uncaused Cause— again. Thinking about it has provided me with a greater understanding of who God is and His important and powerful attributes. Over the years, I have come to realize two of His attributes: energy and knowledge. Energy: that infinite supply from which everything is derived and everything reverts. Knowledge: that infinite supply necessary to shape and form energy into existence.

This morning, my thoughts have taken me back to that fourth-grade project of the triangle representing God in three persons which I call the Uncaused Cause. Although I have identified two of the three apexes as the attributes of energy and knowledge, I constantly struggle to identify the third apex or attribute. Over the years, I have pondered the idea of a being who had all the material resources and knowledge to produce anything and everything. Why would that being, God— the Uncaused Cause— want to create anything that was so inferior to Him? I was still searching for that third apex/attribute of the triangle.

I have always enjoyed making or building things and those activities required three items: 1) supplies and materials; 2) knowledge, information, and a plan; and 3) purpose and a meaning. Being a product of God— the

Uncaused Cause—and made in His image, I felt that He too must have had a reason for creating everything. For a long time, I searched for an understanding of God's reason and purpose for creation. Knowing full well He didn't need a reason, I still held to my conviction that He had one.

This morning's sunrise was one of the best. I was in awe of my surroundings. The trees, the lake, the sky, and all the resplendent colors. I concluded that there must be an infinite amount of beauty. On this morning my question was why? Why would God— the Uncaused Cause— provide to humans who were so much less than Him, this infinite amount of beauty? I thought it must be that beauty is a reflection of His love. An infinite amount of beauty and infinite amount of love.

Now the thought struck me. The answer to my question. God— the Uncaused Cause— had an infinite capacity to love. He had such great love that He had to share it. His loving nature required Him to share His energy and knowledge. I recalled my equilateral triangle from the fourth grade portraying the three persons of God the Father, God the Son, and God the Holy Spirit in one God – the Triune. I now have a fuller appreciation of God. I now equate the person God the Father as the attribute of energy, the person of God the Holy Spirit as the attribute of knowledge, and the person of God the Son as the attribute of infinite love.

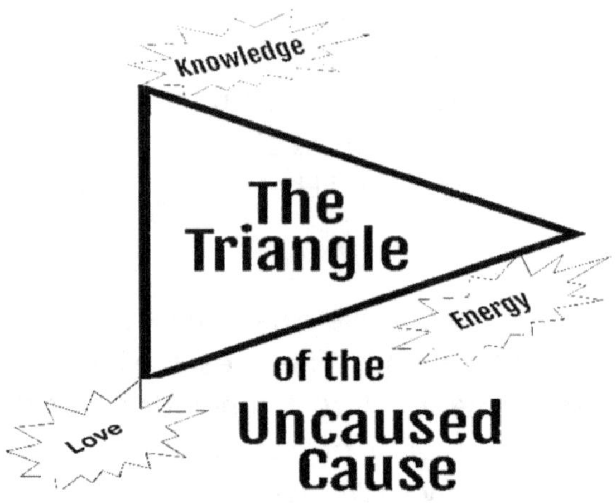

The Complete Triangle

Scientists have tried to trace the beginning of everything to the theory of the Big Bang. But what is the Big Bang? I believe it was more than the beginning of time and matter, but rather was the confluence of infinite energy, knowledge, and love by the Uncaused Cause. Before the Uncaused Cause set everything in motion, time and matter did not exist.

Human beings continue to learn, develop, and discover new knowledge. Are we getting smarter? With the acquisition of new knowledge, we reshape resources and energy to produce things never encountered before. Are we better for it? Over two thousand years ago Jesus Christ came to teach us how to love. Have we advanced in love? What have we learned? Where will we be in the future with infinite energy, knowledge, and love? Like infinite energy and infinite knowledge, infinite love is in everything. Love is the beginning of everything. Without love, nothing would exist. The love of Jesus— the Uncaused Cause of infinite love— is in each of us. Why would he want anything but good for us? Our greatest challenge is to trust in God's plan for us and to unite our will to His will to allow all things to work together towards the good. When we do this, we are filled with peace and tranquility rather than the fear and turmoil we experience when we try to force our will.

My Triangle is now complete.

I have not discarded the traditional Triune of God: Father, Son, and Holy Spirit, but rather combined it with the Triangle of the Uncaused Cause: infinite Energy, Knowledge, and Love, and it has resulted in a deeper understanding and appreciation of the Supreme Being within me.

CHAPTER 48
THE BOOK

Over the course of my life, it appears to me that many people throughout the world have gravitated away from God. And I must confess that during my childhood, my faith was also weakened. However, during my late teens and early 20s, my belief in, and understanding of, a Supreme Being began to change. Eventually, over the span of several years, I began to view the identity of the Supreme Being in a different way. Writing and sharing my understanding and appreciation of the Supreme Being has been an idea of mine for a long time and I felt compelled to share the joy that comes with my understanding. I can't remember exactly when this compulsion began, but I was in my advanced years when I finally put pencil to paper and began writing. I wanted my writing to be factual and sincere. I wanted to express my understanding of the Triangle— three persons in one God. Each time, after a few pages, the words did not seem to communicate my thoughts, so I abandoned the effort. I felt the fully formed concepts in my mind and heart but was unable to convey them. Or just maybe, I was not ready. Maybe I was not prepared to undertake the challenge.

However, the idea never left me and from time to time, I considered beginning again. Occasionally God— The Uncaused Cause— was giving me a nudge. I shared this dilemma with Cindy and she suggested that I talk into a tape recorder. That sounded like a wonderful idea, and I pursued it. However, like my previous attempts at writing, the recordings weren't capturing what I was trying to convey and therefore I again abandoned the project. But the idea still would not go away, I still felt God nudging me toward writing the book. I began to realize being a writer is not easy. I had a story to tell, but writing it was entirely another thing.

After considering some of the books I have read and discussing the situation with Cindy, I decided what I needed was a carrier to communicate my story. Being an old farm boy who loves to make plants flourish and grow, I know they need fertilizer: nitrogen, phosphate, and potash. Whether fertilizer is liquid or solid, it is a biodegradable substance that carries those three elements to the plants. My story needed a carrier. And that carrier was my life. Because at various points in my life I was blessed with the revelation of The Uncaused Cause and the Trinity, my new approach would be a memoir. I would share stories about things that occurred in my life that helped me understand and appreciate the Supreme Being.

My biggest struggle was that although I have had a wonderful life, along the way there were some not so wonderful events. I feared the things I needed to write about might hurt my siblings and their families, my children, and my grandchildren. While I was wrestling with this dilemma, Cindy and I attended a lecture and book signing by Jeannette Walls. I was more excited about going to the Country Club than the presentation, but I decided to read one of her books, *The Glass Castle*, her memoir. The book contained several not so wonderful events about her family.

We arrived early and went to the bar for a cocktail and began socializing with other guests. Cindy and I were introduced to Jeannette Walls. Cindy is very sociable and quickly joined in the conversation. I stood by and listened and smiled for a while, but then my opportunity came. I told Jeannette I read her memoir and that I was writing my memoir. I said that, like her, my life had both wonderful and not so wonderful events. I was curious on her thoughts about addressing the painful events that involved family members. She was very open and forthcoming. She told me to make sure two things occurred: that the writing about the events was truthful and accurate, and that they are part of your story, not someone else's, otherwise remove them. After dinner, Jeannette was introduced as the guest speaker. At the beginning of her talk, she recounted the conversation she just had with me. That made me feel good, and it helped me resolve to continue with my attempt to write this book.

Maybe my previous attempts to write my book were a test to see if it was the will of God. It was now time for me to begin in earnest. God finally gave me more than a nudge, it was more like a kick in the behind. That evening, Cindy and I laid out a plan to set aside an hour for two or three days a week where I would tell her my stories and she would type. The farm accident in which I lost part of my finger was a major hinderance, and in comparison, Cindy is a fast typist.

Before each writing session, we said prayers asking God for guidance and assistance. My first step was to develop a general outline for the book. Next, I identified many of the chapters I would include. I made notes before each session about the chapter and each chapter required several sessions to complete. After completing the draft, the real work began—fleshing out the chapters and removing things that were not part of my story. My motivation in writing *The Triangle of the Uncaused Cause* was to inspire others to come to and have a deeper relationship with the Supreme Being.

It took a long time to write this book. The stories are mine, but how to tell them was revealed to me slowly over many years. I would get ideas at the oddest times – often in the middle of the night. I kept a notepad and pen on my nightstand to scribble them down. Unfortunately, I often could not read what I wrote the next morning. Converting my stories into words was a challenge that I would have been unable to do without God's help and inspiration. At times, I felt it was not even my book, but that I was writing it for Jesus. I believe that God, the Supreme Being— the Uncaused Cause— is infinite energy, knowledge, and love. My hope is that readers will enjoy it, laugh, and maybe even shed some tears. My prayer is to encourage others to explore these ideas and to bring them closer to God— The Uncaused Cause.

EPILOGUE – SUNSET

It is early evening; the beginning of fall and again I am sitting on my porch swing. As the years have passed, I find myself sitting on the swing more often and for longer periods of time. It is rather pleasant. The trees in the forest across the lake on the mountainside are beginning to produce a splendid array of color. It was an unusually wet summer and the abundance of rain brought tremendous growth to the trees and grass.

In past years, I would have mowed the grass for the last time by now. However, this year I anticipate at least a few more mowings being necessary. I mowed today and am now resting on the swing with Petey and a cool glass of sweet tea. Just gently rocking, enjoying the sight and smell of the freshly cut lawn and the beauty of the lake and trees. The sun is getting closer to the horizon, but its rays are still reflecting on the water and highlighting the beautiful colors.

As the sun sets, I also realize that the sun must soon set on what has been my beautiful life even though I have experienced some not so wonderful events from time to time. Throughout my life experiences, I have come to realize that occasionally God— the Uncaused Cause— permits painful things to happen. As humans, we cannot comprehend why this is so. Perhaps God uses the sad or painful events to bring about a good thing. Zeets and I could not understand the many miscarriages, but then God sent us Tina and Tommy to fill the deep pain with indescribable joy. When Zeets died, I was in terrible pain and didn't understand why she was taken away. Then God put Cindy and me together to comfort and care for one another. I believe that the love of God— the Uncaused Cause— is in all things.

I am a goal-oriented person. Whenever I set a goal, I usually find myself making modifications to it. Often I remove goals that no longer seem appropriate. I now realize the fine tuning of my goals was to be in harmony with God's will. Over the years, many of my prayers started in a myopic manner and were requests to receive the results I sought and not necessarily what God— the Uncaused Cause— desired. However, when I expanded the scope of my prayer, God's plans were eventually revealed to me - some of the time. Following God's plan brought harmony into my life; whereas, trying to force my plan resulted in frustration. I need to trust in God's plan for my life.

Now I am focused on one of my few remaining goals in life: to become a Saint and to bring to God— the Uncaused Cause— as many Saints as I can. I want to be in that number when the Saints go marching in! Every night before I fall asleep, I thank Jesus for all the help, assistance, and miracles he has bestowed upon me. Prayer is energy. And because everything comes from energy and the Uncaused Cause is infinite energy, there is no doubt of the power of prayer.

Occasionally, people ask me why I am a Catholic. I always give a two-part answer. First, when I was about two weeks old, my parents had me baptized and raised me in the Catholic faith. Secondly, and more importantly, I am a still a Catholic because of my belief in God— the Uncaused Cause. Jesus is God and Jesus started the Catholic Church.

I address my prayers not only to God the Father, God the Son, and God the Holy Spirit, but also include the Uncaused Cause of Infinite Energy, Infinite Knowledge, and Infinite Love. I have found in Jesus a true friend. Thank you Jesus. Jesus, I love you.

Thank you and God Bless.

ACKNOWLEDGMENTS

Like everything in my life, this book is better because of my wife's involvement. Cindy asked and answered questions, volunteered ideas, and provided constructive love and support. I owe her a debt of gratitude that I can hardly find words to express. Cindy, I thank you so very much. Your loving husband, Tom.

Thank you, Lilei, for asking me, "What was the most memorable event in your life?" As I reflected on it, I realized I had not even addressed it in this book. I went back and wrote about my First Holy Communion.

Thank you, Ann, for being my first reader. It was important to me that my book be scrutinized by a devout Catholic. Thank you for your close reading, constructive comments, and exacting copy editing.

Thank you, Megan, for your IT support.

And above all, thank you, Jesus, for inspiring me with the thoughts and words to use my life story to deliver the message of Your Infinite Love.

About the Author

ABOUT THE AUTHOR

Thomas J. Pojeta is retired and lives in Abingdon, Virginia, with his wife Cindy, dog Petey, and step-cat Baby Martin. He loves spending time with his four grandchildren, "The Buddies," and three bonus grandchildren. He enjoys attending plays at the Barter Theater, driving his pontoon boat on South Holston Lake, and wood turning. Tom is a Fourth Degree Knight of Columbus and part of a close-knit fellowship group at Christ the King Catholic Church. *The Triangle of the Uncaused Cause* is his first book.